IN
CELEBRATION OF

KING'S COLLEGE CHAPEL

Compiled by

Graham Chainey

Published by
The Pevensey Press
for
King's College, Cambridge

First published 1987 © The Pevensey Press and King's College, Cambridge
Edited by Ruth Smith, designed by Tina Dutton; design and production in
association with Book Production Consultants, Cambridge
Typesetting by Goodfellow and Egan; printed in England by The Burlington Press

Acknowledgements

Permission from the following to reprint copyright material is gratefully acknowledged: The Aquarian Press: Nigel Pennick, *The Mysteries of King's College Chapel* (1974); Edward Arnold Ltd: E. M. Forster, *Goldsworthy Lowes Dickinson* (1934); Miss Felicity Ashbee: C. R. Ashbee's journal; the editor of the *Cambridge Evening News*; Cambridge University Press: Kenneth Harrison, *The Windows of King's College Chapel* (1952); Jonathan Cape Ltd: Kingsley Amis, *What Became of Jane Austen?* (1970), and A. S. F. Gow, *Letters from Cambridge* (1945); Jonathan Cape Ltd and the Hugh I'Anson Fausset Estate: Hugh I'Anson Fausset, *A Modern Prelude* (1933); Jonathan Cape Ltd and The Letters of T. E. Lawrence Trust: *The Letters of T. E. Lawrence*, ed. David Garnett (1938); Chatto & Windus Ltd: Shane Leslie, *The Cantab* (1926); Chatto & Windus, The Hogarth Press and the author's estate: Virginia Woolf, *Jacob's Room* (1922) and *A Room of One's Own* (1929); William Collins & Sons Ltd: John Betjeman, *English Cities and Small Towns* (1943), *Selected Letters of E. M. Forster*, ed. Mary Lago and P. N. Furbank (1983), and Hugh Walpole, *The Prelude to Adventure* (Macmillan, 1912); the editor of *Country Life*; Faber & Faber Ltd: Christopher Hassall, *Rupert Brooke: A Biography* (1964), Sylvia Plath, *Letters Home* (1975), and Gwen Raverat, *Period Piece* (1952); Mrs Patricia M. Gill: M. A. Rowley, 'Memories of Childhood in Cambridge'; Harvard University Press: *The Journal of Samuel Curwen, Loyalist*, ed. Andrew Oliver (1972); Her Majesty's Stationery Office: H. M. Colvin in *The History of the King's Works*, I (1963); David Higham Associates Ltd: Charles Causley, *Collected Poems 1951–1975* (Macmillan, 1975); Professor Michael Jaffé; Mr N. J. R. James: M. R. James, 'A Night in King's College Chapel'; Macmillan Ltd: F. E. Hardy, *The Early Life of Thomas Hardy* (1928), and John Julius Norwich, *The Architecture of Southern England* (1985); John Murray Ltd: John Betjeman, *Collected Poems* (1958), and Shane Leslie, *Long Shadows* (1966); Novello & Co Ltd: *Roger North on Music*, ed. J. Wilson (1959); Oxford University Press: Maria Edgeworth, *Letters from England*, ed. Christina Colvin (1971), and *The Letters of William and Dorothy Wordsworth*, II, V, ed. E. de Selincourt (1969, 1979); Penguin Books Ltd: Nikolaus Pevsner, *An Outline of European Architecture* (1943), and *The Buildings of England: Cambridgeshire* (1970), © Nikolaus Pevsner; Mr Bill Powell; the editor of *Private Eye*; Routledge & Kegan Paul Ltd: Francis Woodman, *The Architectural History of King's College Chapel* (1986); Alan Sutton Publishing Ltd: Arthur Oswald in John Harvey and Arthur Oswald, *Medieval English Architects* (1984); Mr Ian Symington: 'Whipplesnaith', *The Night Climbers of Cambridge* (1937); Thames & Hudson Ltd: *Collected Correspondence and London Notebooks of Joseph Haydn*, ed. H. C. Robbins Landon (1959); the editor of *The Times*; A. P. Watt Ltd for the Executors of the Estate of K. S. P. McDowell: E. F. Benson, *David of King's* (1924); Webb & Bower/Macdonald: *The Journeys of Celia Fiennes*, ed. Christopher Morris (1949). Acknowledgments are offered to copyright holders unable to be traced.

ISBN 0 907115 43 8

Preface

KING'S COLLEGE CHAPEL, Cambridge, one of the most perfect buildings in the world, has been admired and discussed for some five
centuries. As early as 1484, while still only half built, it was described by the
University as 'the unparalleled ornament of all England', and the super-
latives have never ceased. Every aspect of it – stone, glass, wood, music – is
of the highest order, their combined survival unique. Begun as a Catholic
Gothic church, completed in the dawn of Protestantism and the English
Renaissance, the Chapel emerged largely unscathed from subsequent
political revolutions and cycles of aesthetic taste, its pre-eminence preserving it alike from Puritan iconoclast and later 'restorer'. Like a ship that has
weathered a perilous voyage, survivor from a shattered fleet, it has come
down to us with its cargo of meaning miraculously intact.

This book collects some of the tributes – and insults – which the Chapel
has elicited over the centuries, together with glimpses into its distinguished
and often picturesque past. For the sake of uniformity I have modernised
and standardised the spelling of quotations; where possible I have arranged
them under the date to which they refer rather than that of composition or
publication.

G.R.C.
Cambridge, 1987

Ut rosa flos florum, sic est domus ista domorum

≈≈≈≈≈≈≈≈≈≈≈≈≈≈≈≈≈≈≈≈≈≈≈≈≈

1441 'THE ROYAL SAINT': *Pious, saintly, humane, liable to depressive stupors, King Henry VI (1421–71) proved better fitted for religious and educational works than to govern a volatile kingdom. Under his rule France was lost, rebellions shook the land, and finally the Wars of the Roses erupted between his Lancastrian faction and that of the rival Yorkists, resulting in his*

Henry VI, after a portrait in one of the Chapel windows (Ackermann's History, *1815).*

deposition in 1461 and murder in 1471. Yet though politically inept he was much loved, miracles were later reported in his name, and two celebrated colleges perpetuate his fame. He founded Eton in 1440, and King's in 1441.

⚜ 1448

THE 'WILL': *A large area of the centre of Cambridge was compulsorily acquired for Henry's new college, though his downfall condemned most of it to stand empty for centuries. In 1448 he signed a document known as his 'Will', in which he formally recorded his designs for Eton and King's. The Chapel at King's was to form the northern range of the main court, with a cloister and tall bell-tower to its west.* He decreed that the Chapel shall contain in length 288 feet of assize without any aisles and all of the wideness of 40 feet, *being* in height 90 feet, embattled, vaulted, and chareroofed [waggon-roofed? leaded?], sufficiently buttressed, and every buttress fined with finials [pinnacles]. *The Chapel as built generally accords with Henry's specifications. In an important sentence, reflecting his ascetic distaste for the more florid architectural decoration of the time, he decreed that* the edification of my same college proceed in large form, clean and substantial, setting apart superfluity of too great curious works of entail [carving] and busy moulding. *Henry had laid the Chapel's foundation stone, beneath the spot intended for the high altar, on St James's Day, 25 July, 1446.*

♔ 1448–61

THE WALLS RISE: *Reginald Ely from Norfolk, the Chapel's first master mason, was granted powers to impress workmen on pain of imprisonment. Stone came by water from Yorkshire and by road from Northamptonshire. The level of the white Yorkshire stone – clearly visible on the Chapel's exterior, stepping down from quite high at the east to a bare few feet at the west – has often been taken as indicating the extent of the Chapel's completion by the time of Henry's deposition; but this is now doubted. The two north-eastern side-chapels alone were vaulted and completed by 1461.*

⚜ 1461–1506

LEAN DAYS: *Little help for a Lancastrian foundation could be expected from a Yorkist king, and at first under King Edward IV work practically stopped. Private subscription enabled a modest resumption in the mid 1470s; the master masons were first John Wolrich and then (from 1477) Simon Clerk. In 1479 Edward relented and granted funds. Even King Richard III, the alleged murderer of Henry VI, continued the payments. By 1485 the five eastern bays had been built and roofed over with timber and lead, but the Antechapel walls had scarcely risen. Then, after Richard's death at*

Bosworth Field, work ceased completely for twenty years. Vainly the college petitioned King Henry VII that the structure magnificently begun by royal munificence now stands shamefully abandoned to the sight. *While Henry, turning the screws of taxation and extortion, amassed a fortune, the scholars of King's lived frugally in the shadow of his uncle's truncated masterpiece.*

♔ 1506

THE PURSE-STRINGS LOOSEN: *On St George's Eve 1506 Henry VII arrived in Cambridge en route to Walsingham, and after robing himself in the Order of the Garter, rode with all his knights to the Chapel* of King's College, which was for the same cause ready appointed with scutcheons [heraldic shields] as is yearly accustomed. *John Fisher, Bishop of Rochester and Chancellor of the University, officiated. These Garter celebrations, usually held at Windsor, may have taken place in the college's temporary chapel, though not impossibly in the unfinished new one. Fisher and the king's mother, Lady Margaret Beaufort (foundress of Christ's and St John's Colleges), were probably as eloquent to the king's ears as the tragic grandeur of the Chapel was to his eyes. Before leaving, he made a first grant of £100 towards continuing the work.*

⚜ 1508–12

A MERITORIOUS WORK PERFECTED: *By spring 1508 construction was back to full pace under the Chapel's fourth and greatest master mason, John Wastell of Bury St Edmunds (architect of the central tower of Canterbury Cathedral). When Henry VII died in 1509, he bequeathed £5000 (equivalent to several hundred times as much in modern terms) for the completion of the Chapel,* that thereby should not be only a notable act and a meritorious work perfected, which else were like to grow to desolation and never to have been done and accomplished, but also divine service there hereafter maintained and supported to the honour and laud of Almighty God. *The money was delivered in the great chest which now stands in the Antechapel to receive contributions towards the Chapel's upkeep. Should the £5000 prove insufficient, Henry's executors were to remit as much more* as shall suffice for the perfect finishing and performing of the same works. *They sent a further £5000 in 1512, by which time the Antechapel had been built and adorned inside and out with stone heraldry showing the donor's arms and supporters. A building begun to the glory of God was being accomplished to the glory of the Tudor dynasty.*

1512–15 THE VAULT: *By a contract signed in about May 1512 it is covenanted, bargained and agreed . . . that the said* John Wastell and Henry Semark shall make and set up or cause to be made and set up at their costs and charges a good sure and sufficient vault for the great Church. *The vault was to be built within three years according to a design already approved by Henry VII's executors. Payment was to be £100 per bay, £1200 for the whole vault. The resulting fan-vaulted stone ceiling, the Chapel's most celebrated architectural feature, combines the greatest visual magnificence with the greatest technical virtuosity. Wastell also undertook to build the Chapel's pinnacles and corner towers (£140 for the pinnacles, £100 per tower), and the vaults in the porches and side-chapels (at prices ranging from £12 to £25). The work apparently went at high speed – not much more than a month per tower, for instance.*

1515–47 THE WINDOWS: *On completion of the stonework, the Royal Glazier, the German-born Barnard Flower, who had already glazed Henry VII's Chapel at Westminster Abbey, was commissioned to install stained glass; but he died in 1517 with only about four windows completed. Then things lapsed; an undated petition to King Henry VIII complained that* the paving, and stalling and glazing . . . is not done for lack of money. *Perhaps as a consequence, in 1526 contracts were drawn up with Galyon Hone, Flower's Flemish successor, and five other London glaziers, to complete the windows within five years with* good, clean, sure and perfect glass and Orient colours and imagery of the story of the old law and of the new law [i.e. the Old and New Testaments]. *By the time of Henry's death in 1547, only the west window was still unglazed. The Antwerp glazier Dierick Vellert, who (being an alien) was not named in the contracts, is now believed to have designed many of the finest scenes.*

1533–8 THE SCREEN: *Anne Boleyn's initials and arms, carved along-side those of her husband, Henry VIII, date the magnificent oak screen to between late 1532, when he married her, and 1536, when he cut off her head. It is not known who carved the screen and stalls, though much of the work seems Continental and it is recorded that around New Year 1535 one 'Philip the carver' dined with other foreigners in the college hall. The stalls were apparently finished by 1538, though the heraldic panels behind them were not added until 1633, and the canopies in 1675–8. The organ, originally built by Thomas Dallam in 1606, has been many times altered and enlarged, most notably by Renatus Harris in 1686–8. The trumpeting angels that now surmount it are Victorian.*

❖ **1544–70**   R ELIGIOUS ROUNDABOUTS: *A high altar, installed in 1544, was removed in 1549 by order of a commission sent down by King Edward VI. At a ceremony in the Chapel, everyone took an oath* for the abolishment of the Bishop of Rome and for the supremacy of the King's Majesty. *But immediately on the accession of the Catholic Queen Mary in 1553,* the whole Popish service, in Latin, was celebrated in King's College, by some zealous men of the house, though contrary to the laws then in force. *The altar was restored. The accession of Queen Elizabeth I in 1558, however, put paid to Catholic hopes and the altar was finally destroyed, although Provost Baker, a Catholic sympathiser, hid the vestments in a vestry until his ejection in 1569. His Puritan successor, Provost Goad, sold them and used the money to install a new college library in the southern side-chapels behind the Choir, where it remained from 1570 until 1828.*

♛ **1564**   Q UEEN ELIZABETH I: *The entire University lined her route to the Chapel's west door, through which, after a lengthy speech from the Public Orator, she entered beneath a canopy borne by the Vice-Chancellor and the three senior Doctors of Divinity. The Chapel's east end had* been hanged with fine tapestry, *and on its south side* was hanged a rich traverse of crimson velvet *to screen her as she sat;* also a fair closet glazed towards the Choir was devised and made in the middle of the roodloft, if the Queen's Majesty perhaps there would repose herself; which was not occupied. *Provost Baker and all the members of the college stood in line along the Antechapel. On entering, she* kneeled down at the place appointed, between the two doors, north and south, the Lady Strange bearing the train. *The Provost kissed her hand, she prayed privately for a moment, then he read aloud a psalm and a collect.* Which done, the whole choir began to sing in English a song of gladness; and so went orderly into their stalls in the Choir. The Queen following, and going into her traverse, under the canopy; and marvellously revising at the beauty of the Chapel, greatly praised it, above all other within her realm.

After evensong the Queen left through a 'privy way' in the northern side-chapels, to stay in the Provost's Lodge. She attended another service the following day, and twice attended plays performed by students in the Antechapel, where a stage had been built. She sat against the south wall beneath a cloth of state, her courtiers either in front of her on a raised platform or on top of the screen. The scene was lit by torches held by Yeomen of the Guard. (John Nichols, *Progresses and Public Processions of Queen Elizabeth,* 1788.)

✠ **1577** NOTABLE PILE: The common schools of Cambridge also are far more beautiful than those of Oxford, only the Divinity School at Oxford excepted, which for fine and excellent workmanship cometh next the mould of the King's Chapel in Cambridge; than the which two, with the Chapel that King Henry the Seventh did build at Westminster, there are not in my opinion made of lime and stone three more notable piles within the compass of Europe. (William Harrison, *The Description of England*.)

♔ **1580** OPPORTUNITY MISSED: If the rest of the house had proceeded according to the Chapel already finished . . . the like college could scant have been found again in any Christian land. (John Stow, *The Chronicles of England*.)

✠ **1598** CAPTURED MANUSCRIPT: A Chapel that may justly claim a place among the most beautiful buildings in the world. On its right side is a fine library, where we saw the *Book of Psalms* in manuscript, upon parchment four spans in length and three broad, taken from the Spaniards at the siege of Cadiz, and thence brought into England with other rich spoils. (Paul Hentzner, *Travels* 1612.) *The college library still possesses the manuscript.*

♔ **1605–6** ORGAN BUILDERS' ACCOUNTS
Item for ebony for the keys 3s 4d
Item for brass for the shaking stop.............................. 4s
Item paid to the Carver for the King's arms
 standing upon the chair organ £3
Item to him for the scutcheons of this College
 and Eton arms 30s
Item paid to Knockle the Limner for laying the said gold etc upon the pipes,
 arms and scutcheons of the chair organ 26s 8d
Item to him for gold and gilding the crowns of the said organ 26s 8d
Item to him for gilding the round towers of the said organ £3
Item for gilding and colouring the brackets............................... 10s
(College accounts.) *Much of the original carving survives, though no longer lavishly gilded.*

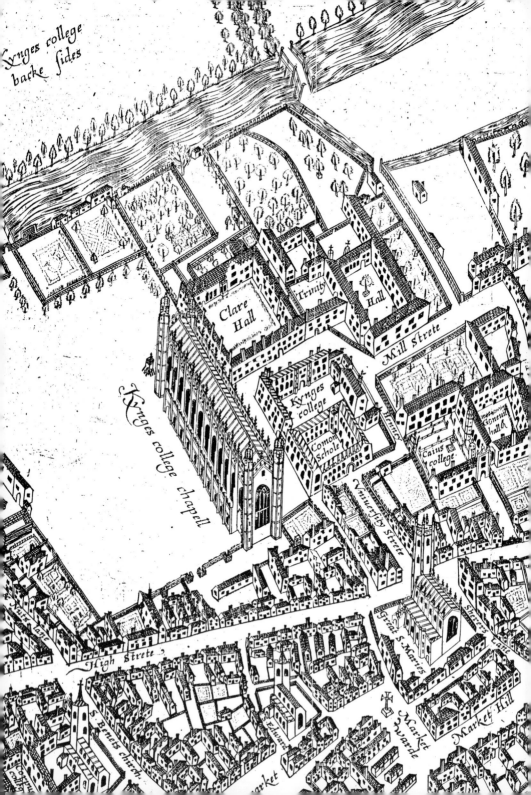

1614 STILL ON HIS CONSCIENCE: To King's College in Cambridge for some cloth or cushions or other ornament for their communion table, pulpit or otherwise in their Chapel, in satisfaction for some injury I did to that place in my indiscreet youth, thereunto drawn by others: £10. (Will of Thomas Singleton, Vice-Chancellor of Oxford University, a student at Clare Hall in the 1560s.)

1622 CHAPEL BEFORE KITCHEN: But that the said Prince's piety might be the more conspicuous, he did not settle the college and finish the kitchen, but first began to build the Chapel, which is so majestic that it claims a place among the most beautiful structures in the world. (Richard Parker, *The History and Antiquities of the University of Cambridge*, 1721 translation.)

1627 FOOTPRINTS IN LEAD: *It was the custom for visitors to have the shape of their foot cut in the leads of the roof, with their name and arms. On 10 March the Duke of Buckingham, favourite of King Charles I and Chancellor of the University,* was on the top of King's College Chapel but refused to have his foot imprinted there as too high for him. (C. H. Cooper, *Annals of Cambridge,* 1842–1908.) *On 27 August when the antiquary Sir Simonds D'Ewes visited Cambridge with his new 13-year-old bride,* we went both up to the top of King's College Chapel, on the south side whereof, upon the leads, my wife's foot was set, being one of the least in England (her age and stature considered), and her arms exsculped within the compass of the foot in a small escutcheon. (*Autobiography and Correspondence,* 1845.)

1629 BADGERS' SKINS: Sir: if mine ability were answerable to mine affection to the worthy Foundations wherein I have received liberal maintenance and education, I would not only bring badgers' skins, but the things of greater value for the adorning and beautifying of the same. But my hope is that God will accept the will, and that your Worship together with the worthy Society will receive with favour what I shall be able to perform. I have sent the workman William Fells, a carver, to view the Chapel and according to his skill to advise what is fit to be done. (Thomas Weaver to the Provost, 20 May.) *The heraldic panels behind the stalls, carved by Fells at Weaver's expense, were installed in 1633. The reference to badgers' skins is unexplained.*

◀ *From John Hamond's view of Cambridge, 1592: note the wooden bell-tower at the west end.*

❦ c.1632 JOHN MILTON
But let my due feet never fail
To walk the studious cloister's pale,
And love the high embowèd roof,
With antique pillars massy proof,
And storied windows richly dight,
Casting a dim religious light.
There let the pealing organ blow,
To the full-voicèd choir below,
In service high, and anthems clear,
As may with sweetness, through mine ear,
Dissolve me into ecstasies,
And bring all heaven before mine eyes.

From 'Il Penseroso', written shortly after Milton finished studying at Christ's College.

♛ 1636 CANNOT SING: In King's College some of the choirmen cannot sing and are divers of them very negligent. The choristers are near one half of them mutes, when they list they come to service with surplices and when they list they come without them. They commonly post [hurry] over their service and perform it with little reverence. Their choristers make no preparation before service be well on, and their song books are very rude and tattered. (Report sent to Archbishop Laud, in C. H. Cooper, *Annals of Cambridge*, 1842–1908.)

❦ 1639 WE CAN DO BETTER: King's College Chapel is a lofty stately building and much beautifies the place. It hath very high and rich windows of scripture stories in coloured glass, done in King Henry the Eighth's time: not so artificial, neat and true as nowadays are made of that kind, as those in Christ Church and Magdalen College in Oxford. (Peter Mundy, *A Petty Progress through some Part of England and Wales*.)

♛ 1642 UNABASHED: *Charles Prince of Wales (the future King Charles II), aged eleven*, went and saw King's Chapel, where at his entrance into the Choir I saw him say his prayers of which he was so little ashamed that in the midst of that multitude he hid not his devotion in his hat. (Joseph Beaumont of Peterhouse, letter home, March.)

⚜ **1643** THE GLASS SPARED: *In August Parliament decreed the abolition from churches of stone altars, altar steps, crucifixes, and all pictures of the Trinity, Virgin Mary, and saints. A widespread destruction of stained glass ensued. William Dowsing, commissioned to enforce the ordinance in the eastern counties, arrived at King's College on 26 December and noted:* Steps to be taken, & 1 thousand Superstitious Pictures ye layder of Christ & theves to goe upon many Crosses, & Jesus write on them. *This has been taken as a threat to the Chapel's glass, the east window in particular. No one has satisfactorily explained the glass's survival. A payment of 6s 8d to Dowsing the following year was not a bribe, as some have claimed, but his survey fee.*

Various legends arose about the glass being taken down and hidden. William Cole (British Library MS, 1742) recorded a story that the west window (in his day still plain) was originally coloured but was broken by the soldiers in the Rebellion, upon which the rest were taken down and hid under the [south] side of the organ loft. *In Sabine Baring Gould's* The Chorister: A Tale of King's College Chapel in the Civil Wars *(1854), one of the choristers assists the Fellows in taking down the glass at night and then, refusing to reveal where it is hidden, is shot by Cromwell's men before the altar. As he dies, his soul flies out of the glassless window like a* delicate ring dove or wood-pigeon.

👑 **1644** USED AS A DRILL HALL: *Cromwell's army sometimes used college buildings for parades in wet weather and* Major-General Crawford, a Presbyterian, made use of King's College Chapel for the purpose, but there is no evidence that any damage was caused to the Chapel. (F. J. Varley, *Cambridge during the Civil War*, 1935.)

Nor was it any whit strange to find whole bands of soldiers training and exercising in the royal Chapel of King Henry the Sixth: nay even the commanders themselves, being commanded to show their new Major General (Crawford) how well they understood their trade, chose that place to train in (whether in policy to conceal their mystery, or out of fear to betray their ignorance, or on purpose to show their soldiers how little God's house was to be regarded, let the world conjecture). (*Querela Cantabrigiensis*, 1646, a royalist propaganda work.)

⚜ **1654** JOHN EVELYN: Afterwards to King's College, where I found the Chapel altogether answered expectation, especially the roof all of stone, which for the flatness of its laying and carving may, I conceive, vie with any in Christendom. The contignation of the roof (which I went upon), weight, and artificial jointing of the stones is admirable. . . From this roof we could descry Ely, and the encampment of Sturbridge Fair now beginning to set up their tents and booths; also Royston, Newmarket, etc. (*Diary*, 31 August.)

♔ **1655** GRAVITY DEFIED: The Chapel in this college is one of the rarest fabrics in Christendom, wherein the stonework, woodwork, and glasswork contend which most deserve admiration. Yet the first generally carrieth away the credit (as being a Stonehenge indeed), so geometrically contrived, that voluminous stones mutually support themselves in the arched roof, as if Art had made them to forget Nature, and weaned them from their fondness to descend to their centre. (Thomas Fuller, *History of the University of Cambridge*.)

⚜ **1660** THE RESTORATION PROCLAIMED: *On 10 May, following the news that Charles II was King, the town band* went up to the top of King's College Chapel, where they played a great while. *Two days later the King was proclaimed at King's College, all the soldiers were placed round on the top of their Chapel from whence they gave a volley of shot.* (C. H. Cooper, *Annals of Cambridge*, 1842–1908.)

♔ **1661** SAMUEL PEPYS: Then to King's College Chapel, where I find the Scholars in their surplices at the service with the organs – which is a strange sight to what it used in my time to be here. (*Diary*, 15 July.) *The organ had been dismantled during the Commonwealth and the choral services suppressed. Pepys had studied at Magdalene College 1651–4.*

⚜ **1672** THROUGH FRENCH EYES: Its outside is ornamented with many little miniatures, and with pyramids, which make it appear as if crowned with flowers. The windows seem to be of chrystal, of every colour, representing the history of the Old Testament; and under them, in bas-relief, are the blazons of the greatest lords of the country, which serve round that fine church like tapestry. Its lobby, or interval between the nave and Choir, is in the fashion of a lattice, covered with leafwork, accompanied by all sorts of fruit and birds, represented according to nature, and so well, that the Principal [Master of St John's], who had, as well as I, made the voyage of Italy, obliged me to acknowledge that nothing more beautiful, or of better workmanship, was to be seen there. The whole

From David Loggan's Cantabrigia Illustrata, *1690: above,* the west front; overleaf, the interior, looking east: note the angel figures on top of the organ (later replaced), the absence of seating in the Antechapel, and the presence of dogs.

...um in Christo Patri ac Domino D^{no} THOMÆ BARLOW Lin... ...colniensi Episcopo, Collegii Regalis in Acad. CANTAB. Juxta vim statuti
...Regis et Fundatoris Illustrissimi Ratione Episcopali pleno Jure... VISITORI Annum Octogesimum secundum, vitæ integritate, morumq suavitate
...ud Theologo non dum defatigato Fidei Orthodoxæ Patrono Summo, hanc... ...ram sancti Viri, et Operis ideo augusti memoriam debita Reverentia... ...Sacelli Delineationem a parte interiori accuratissimam tanquam Pietatis veræ Reg...
D.D.C.Q.   Dav. Logan

of divine service is sung there every day to music. (Jorevin de Rocheford, *Travels*, trans. in *Antiquarian Repertory*, 1809.)

🜲 **1697** CELIA FIENNES: King's College Chapel is the finest building I have heard of. Curious carvings of stone on the outside, twelve large windows and two at each end very large, all finely painted all over the history of the New Testament. It's a hundred and twenty steps to the roof and supported by no pillars, all arch of stone. You walk on the arch, or cradle as it's termed . . . This is a noble building and stands on so advantageous a ground and so lofty built that it's perspicuous above the town. (*The Journeys of Celia Fiennes*, ed. Christopher Morris, 1949.)

⚜ **1700** THE CRADLE: Nothing remarkable till we came within four mile of Cambridge, at which distance the top of King's College Chapel was discernible, appearing in a figure resembling a cradle, and by travellers is so called. (Edward Ward, *A Step to Stirbitch Fair*.)

🜲 **1707** A SPACIOUS TEMPLE: Truly a work of Kings. It is less a Chapel than a spacious and beautiful temple, oblong, lofty, and adorned with the most beautiful carving. Four octagonal towers rise at the corners, topped with domes. The interior is vaulted, and the whole of this great building is so skilfully constructed that the vault needs no pillars. The Choir is separated from the nave by a screen whose workmanship matches all the rest and on which rests a fine organ case with statues of two angels blowing trumpets and of King David playing his harp. (James Beeverell, *Les Délices de la Grande Bretagne*.) *The original trumpeting angels were replaced in the 1730s by Gothic pinnacles, which were in turn replaced in 1860.*

⚜ **1710** NO MIRACLE: It is certainly an incomparably elegant building of stone, especially as regards the quantity of carved work about it. But it is no such miracle as it is made out to be in the *Délices d'Angleterre*, that it is without pillars, for, though long and lofty, it is not at all broad. We heard the sermon, and admired exceedingly the goodness of the organ; for it is small, and yet of a deep and extremely pleasant tone. (Zacharias Conrad von Uffenbach, in J. E. B. Mayor, *Cambridge under Queen Anne*, 1911.)

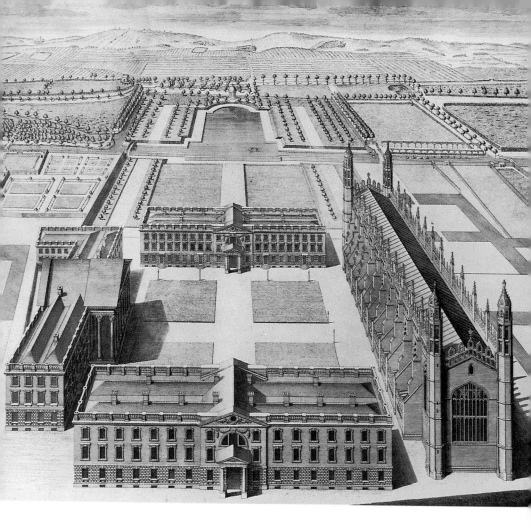

✠1714 LITTLE BENEFIT: I forgot to note that I was at the most stately fabric in the University, viz., King's College Chapel, where I got little benefit by the prayers, because of the music and noble architecture, which too much diverted my thoughts. (Ralph Thoresby, antiquary of Leeds, *Diary*, 7 July.)

⚜1714 OXFORD UNRUFFLED: Though King's College Chapel exceeds any of our chapels, yet when we excel them on so many other accounts, it will not (as I take it) be proper from this only building to think that that University may be compared with ours. (Thomas Hearne, Oxford antiquary, to B. Willis, 17 November.)

ᔕᔕ ᔕᔕ ᔕᔕ ᔕᔕ ᔕᔕ ᔕᔕ ᔕᔕ ᔕᔕ ᔕᔕ

◀ *Gibbs's unfulfilled design for completing the court, engraved by Essex, 1741.*

1725 BEAUTY TRAP
Mixed with the gazing crowd I hither come,
Nor dreamt destruction near this sacred dome;
Where holy hymns, and solemn songs of praise,
A venerable adoration raise;
But with surprise, at once I hear and see
A speaking, and a silent harmony.
Transporting sounds! My fainting senses rise,
Winged with the sweeter music of your eyes.
(William Pattison, 'To a Lady at King's College Chapel', *Poetical Works*, 1728.)

1727 DANIEL DEFOE: The royal chapel at Windsor, and King's College Chapel, at Cambridge, are indeed very gay things, but neither of them can come up to the minster of York on many accounts. (*A Tour through the Whole Island of Great Britain.*)

1727 JAMES GIBBS: A beautiful building of the Gothic taste, but the finest I ever saw. (*A Book of Architecture.*)

1728 CRUSHED: *The college's peal of bells, originally donated by the Founder, had hung for centuries in a temporary wooden clochard to the west of the Chapel; this had become dangerously ruinous.* In December Henry West, bellringer of King's College, was crushed to death by one of the five great bells of that college. (C. H. Cooper, *Annals of Cambridge*, 1842–1908.) *The clochard was demolished in 1739, after which the bells stood in the Antechapel until their sale for scrap metal in 1754.*

c.1728 QUINTESSENCE OF HARMONY: Between the shell of the main arches and the timber covering, lay an ear to one of the holes through which cords pass for carrying chairs when the inside of the roof is cleaned, and the organ with the choir sounding, such a delicious music shall be heard, as I may call the quintessence of harmony, not otherwise to be described. (*Roger North on Music*, ed. John Wilson, 1959.)

The former clochard (from J. J. Raven, The Church Bells of Cambridgeshire, *1881).*

✾ **1735**　IMPERTINENT: The King's Chapel is amazing, not so much for the greatness of the work, though truly great, as for a lightness and elegancy beyond any Gothic structure in my knowledge. One should think the carving was but newly done, it looks so fresh; and if it was not for the most impertinent music gallery which cuts it in two, and destroys the unity of the design, it might perhaps have as magnificent an aspect as any old building in Europe. (Thomas Blackwell, Professor of Greek at Aberdeen, to Roger Gale, 2 October.)

1738

ROMANTICISM BORN: *Already as a student at King's in the 1730s, Horace Walpole evinced his (then unfashionable) love of Gothic architecture*:

> When Henry bade this pompous Temple rise,
> Nor with presumption emulate the skies,
> Art and Palladio had not reached the land,
> Nor methodized the Vandal builder's hand.
> Wonders unknown to rule these piles disclose;
> The walls as if by inspiration rose . . .
> Sweet strains along the vaulted roof decay,
> And liquid Hallelujahs melt away;
> The floating accents lessening as they flow,
> Like distant arches gradually low.

('Verses in Memory of King Henry the Sixth', *Fugitive Pieces*, 1758.)

1743

HABEMUS PRAEPOSITUM! *Following the death of Andrew Snape – said to have suffered* from attacks of the gout so frequent and severe that he had to be carried into Chapel in a sedan chair and lifted into his stall – *the Fellows met to choose a new Provost*. The Fellows went into Chapel on Monday morning before noon in the morning as the statute decrees. After prayers and sacrament they began to vote – 22 for George; 16 for Thackeray; 10 for Chapman. Thus they continued, scrutinizing, and walking about, eating, and sleeping; some of them smoking. Still the same numbers for each candidate; till yesterday about noon (for they held that in the 48 hours allowed for the election no adjournment could be made) when the Tories, Chapman's friends, refusing absolutely to concur with either of the two other parties, Thackeray's votes went over to George by agreement, and he was declared.

A friend of mine, a curious man, tells me he took a survey of his brothers at the hour of two in the morning, and that never was a more curious, or a more diverting spectacle. Some wrapped in blankets, erect in their stalls like mummies; others, asleep on cushions, like so many Gothic tombs. Here a red cap over a wig; there a face lost in the cape of a rug. One blowing a chafing dish with a surplice sleeve; another warming a little negus, or sipping Coke upon Littleton, i.e. tent and brandy. Thus did they combat the cold of that frosty night, which has not killed any one of them, to my infinite surprise. (Daniel Wray of Queens' College, 19 January, in John Nichols, *Literary History of the Eighteenth Century*, 1817. *Negus: mulled wine, usually port or sherry; tent: low-alcohol Spanish wine*.)

If I remember right they were three days and nights confined . . . and had their beds, close-stools etc. with them, and their commons etc. given them in at the windows. (Edmund Carter, *History of the University of Cambridge*, 1753.)

♛ **1749** FOUND ON A DUNGHILL: Last Thursday morning about eleven o'clock, two little boys being at play on a dunghill near Parker's Piece, found the first joint of one of the silver candlesticks which were stole out of King's College Chapel; and about two in the afternoon the same boys found another joint; both which pieces are now in the custody of Mr Alderman Yorke. This week a woman, dressed in man's apparel, was stopped in London offering to sale a part of one of the above candlesticks; and being carried before a Justice, was committed to the New Gaol, Southwark. (*Cambridge Journal and Weekly Flying Post*, 15 July.) *The magnificent candlesticks that stood on either side of the altar had been donated by Provost Page, 1668–9. Mary Stubbs, who stole them on the night of 13 July 1749, was tried in August* in man's clothes *and sentenced to transportation to the West Indies.*

⚜ **1753** EXTRAORDINARY MUSIC: [It] is the only public Chapel in town, and on a Sunday afternoon (especially in the summer time and fine weather) you may see it well filled, and amongst them numbers of ladies. Here is a sermon every Lady Day, and extraordinary music, when they commemorate their Founder and benefactors; and till within these few years, after sermon, the music used to go up to the leads of the Chapel and there perform. (Edmund Carter, *The History of the University of Cambridge*.)

♔ **1762** WREN IMPRESSED: A work, alone sufficient to ennoble any age . . . There is a tradition that Sir Christopher Wren went once a year to survey the roof of the Chapel of King's College, and said that if any man would show him where to place the first stone, he would engage to build such another. (Horace Walpole, *Anecdotes of Painting in England*.)

⚜ **1763** CAPTURED COLOURS: On Wednesday last the nine colours taken by General Draper at Manila were carried in procession to King's Chapel by the Scholars of the college, accompanied by the Fellows, the organ playing and the choir singing Te Deum and preceding them. The colours were erected on each side of the altar rails, where the Rev. Mr Barford, Public Orator of the University and one of the Fellows, spoke a Latin oration; after which followed the evening service and a thanksgiving anthem. (*Cambridge Chronicle*, 7 May 1763.) *The Spanish colours, captured by Sir William Draper, former Fellow of the college, were later moved to the Antechapel, near the organ loft; in 1773, having become dirty and ragged, they were put away in a side-chapel. They survived until 1949 when, found on top of a bookcase and unrolled, they disintegrated.*

1765 NARROW ESCAPE: By the violence of the wind on Wednesday morning, one of the pinnacles of the south-west turret of King's College Chapel was blown down and fell with such amazing force as to penetrate near four feet into the gravel walk. Several persons were within a few yards of the spot, but providentially no one received any hurt. (*Cambridge Chronicle*, 16 March.)

1769 CLAUSTROPHOBIA: King's College Chapel gives us on the *outside* a very beautiful form: *within*, though it is an immense and noble aisle, presenting the adjunct idea of lightness and solemnity, yet its disproportion disgusts. Such height and such length, united by straitened parallels, hurt the eye. You feel immured. Henry the [Seventh], we are told, spent twelve hundred pounds in adorning the roof. It is a pity he had not spent it in widening the walls. We should then have had a better form, and should have been relieved from the tedious repetition of roses and port-cullises, which are at best but heavy and unpleasing ornaments. (William Gilpin, *Observations on Several Parts of the Counties of Cambridge, Norfolk, Suffolk and Essex*, 1809.)

1769 MARIOLATRY: In the middle of one of these roses (on the west side, towards the south) may be seen a small figure of the Virgin Mary: after which foreigners make frequent enquiries, and never fail to pay it a religious reverence; crossing their breasts at the sight, and addressing it with a short prayer. (Henry Malden, *An Account of King's College Chapel*.) *Malden, the dissolute Chapel Clerk, did not write the book attributed to him (the first guidebook to the Chapel). It was compiled by a charitable undergraduate, with help from one of the Fellows, to support Malden's destitute widow and children.*

Work in progress during the second major restoration, in 1968.

⚜ 1775   FIRST MAJOR RESTORATION: On Friday March 24 1775, King's College Chapel (which has been shut up eleven months for the purpose of building a new altarpiece, paving the greater part of the Chapel, and making other decorations) was opened with Divine Service, and a Latin oration by Mr Rennel, one of the Scholars of the college. This structure, so justly esteemed by connoisseurs the most perfect monument of Gothic architecture, receives no inconsiderable ornament from the present improvements. The pavement of the Antechapel is plain and uniform, exhibiting fully to the view a spacious and beautiful area. The Choir, which has been lengthened by the space of a window [i.e. the altar moved back to the east wall], is paved with new marble from the end of the stalls; and the whole east end of the Chapel, with the altar (which has been left unfinished since the reign of Henry VII) is now completed in a style peculiarly corresponding to the simplicity and magnificence of the building. (*Cambridge Chronicle*, 25 March.) *The architect was James Essex. His 'Gothick' reredos rather inappropriately echoed the Chapel's exterior stonework, and he inserted on either side of the east window large stone niches that seemed, according to one critic,* only to require the insertion of two gigantic idols in order to complete their obtrusive vulgarity. *The new floor pattern in the eastern three bays was also inferior to that of 1702. Provost Hacomblen's lectern was ejected from the Choir. In 1780 the Earl of Carlisle presented for altarpiece a* Deposition *attributed then to the Italian artist Daniele da Volterra but now to his contemporary Girolamo Siciolante da Sermoneta (1512–80).*

1776 CAPITAL: Bill and myself went after breakfast and saw King's Chapel, the finest I ever saw, all fine carved stone, the roof of the same – most capital piece of architecture indeed; gave a man that showed it to us 1s. (James Woodforde, *Diary of a Country Parson*, ed. J. Beresford, 1924–31.)

1777 AMERICAN TOURIST: From hence we proceeded to King's College Chapel; for a description must refer to the book bought in it. *Samuel Curwen, merchant from Salem, particularly admired on the screen* a representation of God the Father driving down the rebellious angels, on whose faces the expression of distress, anguish and dismay is inimitable and most just. (*The Journal of Samuel Curwen, Loyalist*, ed. Andrew Oliver, 1972.)

1777 MONKISH LONGINGS: I dote on Cambridge, and could like to be often there. The beauty of King's College Chapel, now it is restored, penetrated me with a visionary longing to be a monk in it. (Horace Walpole to William Cole, 22 May.)

1779 CONVERTED: *In his first term at King's Charles Simeon, later to become Vice-Provost and a celebrated Cambridge Evangelical preacher, was disturbed to learn that he would have to attend a communion service.* Satan himself was as fit to attend as I, *he felt, and spent the next weeks desperately trying to prepare himself, rather than* eat and drink my own damnation. *As a result, on Easter Sunday,* I awoke early with those words upon my heart and lips, 'Jesus Christ is risen today! Hallelujah! Hallelujah!' From that hour peace flowed in rich abundance into my soul, and at the Lord's table in our Chapel I had the sweetest access to God through my blessed Saviour. (Charles Simeon, *Memoirs*, ed. W. Carus and R. Carter, 1847.)

1787 FIRST SIGHT OF IT
It was a dreary morning when the wheels
Rolled over a wide plain o'erhung with clouds,
And nothing cheered our way till first we saw
The long-roofed Chapel of King's College lift
Turrets and pinnacles in answering files
Extended high above a dusky grove.
(William Wordsworth, *The Prelude*, Book III, 1850.)

1789 LIKE A BIRD OF PARADISE: So you was not quite satisfied, though you ought to have been transported, with King's College Chapel, because it has no aisles like every common cathedral. I suppose you would object to a bird of paradise because it has no legs, but shoots to heaven in a trait, and does not rest on earth. Criticism and comparison spoil many tastes; you should admire all bold and unique essays that resemble nothing else. The *Botanic Garden*, the *Arabian Nights*, and King's Chapel are above all rules; and how preferable is what no one can imitate to all that is imitated, even from the best models! (Horace Walpole to Mary Berry, 30 June.)

1789 DÉJÀ VU: I wish I could think as an old sexton did at King's College; one of the Fellows told him he must get a great deal of money by showing it – 'Oh! no, master,' replied he, 'everybody has seen it now.' (Horace Walpole to Lady Ossory, 23 August.)

1791 FRANZ JOSEPH HAYDN: The King's Chapel is famous because of its stuccoed ceiling. It is all of stone, but so delicate that nothing more beautiful could have been made of wood. It is already 400 years old, and everyone thinks that it is not more than 10 years old, because of the firmness and peculiar whiteness of the stone. (*Collected Correspondence and London Notebooks of Joseph Haydn*, ed. H. C. Robbins Landon, 1959.)

1792 LIKE IVORY: What shall I say of King's Chapel? You will scarcely find anything like it in Europe in this taste. Imagine a building 291 feet long, 45 feet broad, and 78 feet high, all built in the noblest style, and as carefully finished as a piece of ivory carving. It is difficult to conceive how the wide stone vault is supported, and it only becomes intelligible when you see the exterior; for in the interior there are no pillars. The light that falls through the lofty windows, which are painted in the most glorious colours, has something solemn about it, and when you stand by the altar and look down the whole length of the building, with the last rays of the setting sun pouring through the open door – I cannot say what I felt in that moment, but I learnt that it is possible for art and sublime nature to harmonize in one. (Friedrich Wilhelm von Hassell, German traveller, in *King's College Chapel: Comments and Opinions*, 1956.)

1793 SEDITION: Damn the monarchy; I want none; I wish to see all the churches down, and the roads mended with them, and King's Chapel made a stable of. (John Cook of Petty Cury, baker; *Cambridge Chronicle*, 20 July.) *Cook was sent to prison.*

1800 UNDIMINISHED: I was curious to ascertain whether the Gothic architecture of Henry [VI] Chapel would please me now, as it did many years ago, long before I saw the wonders of Italy. I found time and comparison had not in the least diminished my admiration of it. (*The Journal of Elizabeth Lady Holland*, 1908.)

1800 ROBBERY: Grimshaw had, early in the spring, secured a key of the outer door of the Chapel, by which the two confederates admitted themselves for several nights, and worked without interruption on the different locks that stood between them and their projected booty; many of these locks being very antique, and of an unusual construction, put Kidman's ingenuity several times to the rack . . . Grimshaw in despair relinquished his part of the undertaking, alleging to his comrade 'that the place looked so awful, that he trembled every time as if he had the ague'. The panic was communicated. *Kidman however soon returned, conquered the last lock and made off with the valuable collection of coins and medals kept in the muniment room (now the Memorial Chapel). He and Grimshaw were caught in 1801; Grimshaw was hanged, Kidman was transported to Australia.* (*The Trials of W. Grimshaw and R. Kidman for Burglary*, 1801.)

♛ **1805** CAPRICIOUS: No part of the interior of King's Chapel is unornamented; and though the ornaments, considered with reference to parts only, often appear crowded, capricious, and unmeaning, yet the effect of the whole together is more rich, grand, light and airy than that of any other building known, either ancient or modern. (Richard Payne Knight, *An Analytical Enquiry into the Principles of Taste*.)

⚜ **1805** SHOWN ROUND BY SIMEON: He took me into King's College Chapel, that celebrated building. He told me that he had lately compared the size of it with the dimensions of Noah's Ark as given in the Scripture, and found that the Ark was twice the length, and twice the breadth, and two-thirds the height of the Chapel. The altarpiece was put up about 23 years ago and is said to be by Daniele da Volterra but it is an inferior performance . . . Mr Simeon said that he remembered being impressed with the representation thus before him while he was receiving the Holy Sacrament. This caused me to ask him whether such reproductions might not assist devotion. He did not seem disposed to admit it. He said proper devotion must arise from another feeling. (Joseph Farington, *Diary*, ed. James Greig, 1924.) *For Simeon see 1779.*

ᔆᔆᔆᔆᔆᔆᔆᔆᔆᔆᔆᔆᔆᔆ

1806 VARYING ASPECTS: A more commanding elevation than that of this Chapel, seen from the Senate House, will not be found in any other part of the English dominions . . . From the opposite walks, beyond the river, the elevation of the west end, with its vast window, its portico, and lofty turrets rising from a certain advantage of ground, is indeed more richly picturesque. (James Dallaway, *Observations on English Architecture*.)

1807 PERFECTION AND DECLINE: Perhaps the only specimen in which the perfection and decline of what has been absurdly termed the Gothic style may be completely seen. In the eastern part of the structure, we have the most elegant and pure example of the art. Here decoration is sufficient, without profusion . . . The western part of the

Varying aspects: opposite, the College and the Senate House from King's Parade, by Thomas Malton, 1798, with the old Provost's Lodge between the Chapel and the street; below, the College from the Backs, from J. Le Keux's Memorials of Cambridge, *1841.*

building, though executed in the same style, is rather too much incumbered with ornament; and the woodwork screen which separates the Chapel into two parts serves only to show that the good taste which guided the original architect, a century before, had departed in the days of Henry the Eighth. (John Britton, *The Architectural Antiquities of Great Britain*.)

♔ 1809 DISFIGURED: Walked to King's College Chapel. The small towers on the outside very light and beautiful. The inside struck me much more than it did in the year 1786 [1789?], when I first saw it. I did not feel so much the want of the intersecting arches of aisles as I remember I did then. It is disfigured by an organ loft of the worst style of Henry VIII; sort of sprigged pilasters. The painted glass windows very fine. The east window, though very large, not remarkable for the beauty of its tracery. (Mary Berry, *Journal and Correspondence*, 1865.)

⚜ 1810 VERTIGO: After dinner I went to King's College Chapel, a most beautiful Gothic building with a very long roof supported without pillars on the inside. The windows are all, except one, of the finest painted glass. Mr Clarkson did not go with me; and my guide persuaded me to go to the top of the building, where I had a fine view of all the colleges and the town. When I found myself there alone with that stranger an odd fright came upon me I seemed to be so completely in his power, he might, as I thought, have done what he pleased with me and nobody could have seen or heard or done anything about it. This was very foolish and after sitting down a little while I got the better of it. Perhaps my dizziness from mounting to so great a height might be the main cause of this feeling – for the young man was very civil and modest enough. (Dorothy Wordsworth to Mrs Cookson, 29 August.)

♛ 1813 MUSIC VERSUS MECHANICS: Now to the beauty of Cambridge, the beauty of beauties! – King's College Chapel! I had seen prints of it in Britton, and had heard much of it from many of its admirers; but it far surpassed my expectations . . . no engraved representation can give an idea of the effect of size, height and *continuity* of grandeur in the whole building . . . Your friend took us up the hundred stairs to the roof – where *he* was delighted with the sound of the organ and the chaunting, rising from the choir below, and my father was soon absorbed in the contemplation of the mechanical wonders of the roof . . . Mr Smedley

The interior of the roof, showing the upper side of the stone vault and the timbers of the outer roof (R. Backhouse, Cambridge University Almanack, *1833).*

exclaimed 'Is not the sound of the organ fine?' To which my father, at cross purposes, answered, speaking to Mrs E., 'Yes – the iron was certainly added afterwards.' Mr Smedley at once confessed that he had no knowledge or taste for mechanics; but he had the patience and good nature to walk up and down this stone platform three quarters of an hour . . . At last, to Mr Smedley's great joy, he got my father alive off this roof. (Maria Edgeworth to her brother, 1 May.)

⚜ 1814 A HERO'S WELCOME: The [Senate House] ceremonies being concluded, [General] Blücher with his *cortège* was conducted to King's Chapel, on entering which he was saluted with a grand overture on the organ, accompanied by double drums, and a full chorus. This scene was unspeakably gratifying. Professor Marsh, who speaks German with great fluency, explained to the Marshal the beauties of that sublime edifice, which he contemplated with evident delight, making repeated inquiries respecting the principle of its construction. (*A Narrative of the Celebration of Peace at Cambridge.*)

👑 **1814** PATCHES ON GREATNESS: Still, it must be confessed, some littlenesses and human weaknesses are too obvious: I mean those minute devices of the arms of the York and Lancastrian Houses, with roses, portcullises, fleurs de lis, and crowns. These little patches on greatness, these vain mementos of magnificence, which would not be forgotten, these heterogeneous intermixtures, and obtrusive impertinencies of royal heraldic trifling with divine combinations, religiously considered, are quite out of place; and, architecturally, are the very opposite to sublimity and grandeur. (George Dyer, *History of the University and Colleges of Cambridge*.)

⚜ **1815** MAGIC ART: This magnificent structure is the greatest ornament, not only of this college, but of the University; and indeed, considered as a whole, it cannot be paralleled by any edifice in

The 'patches on greatness' objected to by Dyer: the Tudor rose, Beaufort portcullis, and arms and supporters of Henry VII emblazoning the west wall.

the world in beauty of Saracenic architecture. The massy strength and airy lightness of its roof were never equalled. Here, indeed, we perceive not only the operation of a master artist, but almost of magic art. The roof looks as if cut at once by an invisible power out of a solid quarry of stone. (Rudolf Ackermann, *A History of the University of Cambridge*.)

♛ **c.1815–19** CHIVALRY REVIVED: As an undergraduate he resolved to be a knight, and getting into King's College Chapel at nightfall, kept his vigil there till dawn. (Bernard Holland, *Memoir of Kenelm Henry Digby*, 1919.)

⚜ **1817** SACRILEGE: On Saturday night or early on Sunday morning King's College Chapel was broken open and the two silver candlesticks taken from the altar. The small door near the east end of the Chapel was forced open to effect this sacrilegious robbery. A liberal reward has been offered for the detection of the offender or offenders, but hitherto without success. (*Cambridge Chronicle*, 24 January.) *The candlesticks stolen replaced those stolen in 1749. The entrance through the east wall of the north-eastern side-chapel was blocked up later that year.*

👑 **1818** ENCRUSTED WITH DUST: If, after encountering the summer's heat and winter's frost of nearly three centuries, and many parts of them being also *encrusted* with the accumulated dust of that long period, these windows still appear unrivalled, what must have been the beauty of the *nudities,* and the brilliancy of the colours, when they were first put up? (J. K. Baldrey, *A Dissertation upon the Windows of King's College Chapel.*)

⚜ **1820** WILLIAM WORDSWORTH
Tax not the royal Saint with vain expense,
With ill-matched aims the Architect who planned –
Albeit labouring for a scanty band
Of white-robed Scholars only – this immense
And glorious Work of fine intelligence!
Give all thou canst; high Heaven rejects the lore
Of nicely-calculated less or more;
So deemed the man who fashioned for the sense

These lofty pillars, spread that branching roof
Self-poised, and scooped into ten thousand cells,
Where light and shade repose, where music dwells
Lingering – and wandering on as loth to die;
Like thoughts whose very sweetness yieldeth proof
That they were born for immortality.

What awful pérspective! while from our sight
With gradual stealth the lateral windows hide
Their Portraitures, their stone-work glimmers, dyed
In the soft chequerings of a sleepy light.
Martyr, or King, or sainted Eremite,
Who'er ye be, that thus, yourselves unseen,
Imbue your prison-bars with solemn sheen,
Shine on, until ye fade with coming Night!
But from the arms of silence – list! O list!
The music bursteth into second life;
The notes luxuriate, every stone is kissed
By sound, or ghost of sound, in mazy strife;
Heart-thrilling strains, that cast, before the eye
Of the devout, a veil of ecstasy!

('Inside of King's College Chapel, Cambridge', *Ecclesiastical Sonnets* 43–4,
1822.)

👑 c.1822–5　COMPULSORY CHAPEL: We had Chapel at 8 – our
great grievance, as no Chapels were allowed us, and it
was so monotonous to get up every morning at 8. The authorities had no
doubt felt this, and had provided a relief. It was in the form of a Latin
epigram of four lines, in which utter grief was usually expressed at the
power of sleep, and the regret which must be felt by the Dean at our
absence. The same epigram was sufficient for the whole three years of
residence. In the fervour of a first term I had composed two – which were
submitted alternately with the regularity of a loom. (William Tucker, *King's
Old Court*, c.1895.) *From the 1870s the obligation to produce an epigram was
replaced by the requirement to sign in at 8 o'clock at the Porter's lodge;
compulsory Chapel was abolished in 1912.*

⚜ 1825　CORMORANT TAKEN: On Wednesday afternoon, the 17th
inst., a cormorant alighted on the top of the south-west turret
of King's College Chapel, and being observed by the chapel clerk, he went

up the opposite turret, and shot it. The bird instantly flew across the market hill, when it fell on a house, and was taken, but died in a short time. (*Cambridge Chronicle*, 26 August.) *Another cormorant, which roosted on the same turret in 1906, was also shot.*

♛ **1827** WOODWORK REGRETTABLE: King's College Chapel as a Perpendicular building, if it yields to any in the kingdom, yields only to St George's Chapel, Windsor; it has one advantage, it remains unaltered and entire, unpatched, unmodernized, uninjured . . . That in such a building such an organ screen, such stalls, and such tabernacle work should have been suffered to have been erected, is a matter of equal astonishment and regret. (G. R. Boissier, *Notes on the Cambridgeshire Churches*.)

⚜ **1827** PEPPER-BOXES AND SNOBBESSES: This magnificent temple is one of the wonders of the world. It is said by travellers in many respects to have no parallel . . . It is decorated with four pinnacles resembling, *si magna componere parvis*, so many gigantic pepperboxes . . . At this Chapel there is cathedral service every day, at three o'clock; to hear the chanting and anthem of which many gownsmen and others attend, promenading the spacious Antechapel. On Sundays . . . we have also a pretty sprinkling of the lady-snobbesses, who go likewise (emphatically be it understood) to see and be seen. (J. M. F. Wright, *Alma Mater: Or Seven Years at the University of Cambridge*.) *Snob: University slang for a townsman.*

♛ **c.1828–31** CHARLES DARWIN: I acquired a strong taste for music, and used very often to time my walks so as to hear on weekdays the anthem in King's College Chapel. This gave me intense pleasure, so that my backbone would sometimes shiver. I am sure that there was no affectation or mere imitation in this taste, for I used generally to go by myself to King's College, and I sometimes hired the chorister boys to sing in my rooms. Nevertheless I am so utterly destitute of an ear, that I cannot perceive a discord, or keep time and hum a tune correctly; and it is a mystery how I could possibly have derived pleasure from music. (*Life and Letters of Charles Darwin*, 1887.)

⚜ **1833** S.T. COLERIDGE: The principle of the Gothic architecture is infinity made imaginable. It is, no doubt, a sublimer effort of genius than the Greek style; but then it depends much more on execution for its effect. I was more than ever impressed with the marvellous sublimity and transcendent beauty of King's College Chapel. It is quite unparalleled. (*Table Talk*, 1835.)

👑 **1835** EXECUTION RUDE: If the exterior makes a very satisfactory impression, the effect of the interior is highly surprising and agreeable . . . It inspires in an extraordinary degree a sensation of sublimity, and yet at the same time of lightness and cheerfulness . . . The Crucifixion, a large painting on glass which fills one of the end windows, is said to be after a design by Holbein. The execution however is so rude that there is no trace of his spirit. (G. F. Waagen, Director of the Royal Gallery, Berlin, *Works of Art and Artists in England*, 1838.)

⚜ **1836** A KING'S BOY: On the 7th of July, 1836, I became a King's boy, was introduced to a 'Bishop' (tailor) on the corner of St Edward's Passage, on King's Parade, and was measured for my first gown. Father had to take me to a hatter for a top hat (my! what an expense those hats were, the *wear* being of short duration) . . . We had salary, payable quarterly, two quarters at six shillings and fourpence, and two quarters at two shillings and sixpence – nearly eighteen shillings per annum – parents finding all our clothing and food excepting dinner . . . Upon leaving the choir there was a sum of money – 'Box Money' – from an accumulated fund, given for the purpose of apprenticeship, according to the number of years' service. (Thomas H. Case, *Memoirs of a King's College Chorister*, 1899.)

👑 **1836–45** IRREVERENCE: Glorious old pile! after sixty-two years I feel an influence stealing over me indescribable with a sense of awe when I picture the irreverence that used to be a common custom . . . With horror I have many times called to mind the fifteenth evening of the month (the psalm having seventy-three verses) when most irreverent words have been hissed in some of our ears spurring us up not to

◀ *Looking west from the sanctuary (from J. and H. S. Storer,* Delineations of the Chapel of King's College, *c.1830).*

'drag' . . . I have heard conversations carried on during the intonation of the Creeds that would shock in a great degree, I hope, the vast majority of those attending these services at this time . . . Dear old King's Chapel, would God that every undevout incident connected [with you?] could be entirely obliterated, and every Heavenly and good one be immovably grafted in my very being. (*Ibid.*)

SPURS: An old custom was just dying out upon my advent, viz., when a military man appeared in Chapel with spurs he was approached with some authority or bombast, and a fee or fine was demanded as a safeguard for his spurs. (*Ibid.*)

JACKDAWS' EGGS: Many were found upon the wall plates and other spots inside the roof, but some could be got, at great risk, from the gutter or heads of stack pipes, and a very tempting nest caused a very foolhardy action. Not able to reach low enough through the battlements in the ordinary way, one hung almost suspended clear of the battlements, held by the legs and feet by the other two, and thus procured the four eggs, handing them up one at a time. (*Ibid.*)

❧ 1836 SIMEON'S FUNERAL: On entering the west door of the Chapel, I was struck by the multitude of persons who filled the nave – men, women, and children; all, so far as I observed, in mourning, and very many giving proof that they were real mourners by their sighs and their tears. These I understood to be the hearers and [Holy Trinity Church] parishioners of Mr Simeon, who had been permitted to attend; and through this sorrowing crowd the procession moved on into the Choir . . . The Provost read most impressively; and, taking under review all the circumstances and accompaniments of the funeral – the affectionate respect for the departed, himself the Luther of Cambridge – the sorrowing multitudes, including several hundreds of University men – the tones of the organ, more solemn than ever I heard them – the magnificence of the building – I should think that no person who was present would ever fail, so long as he remembers anything, to carry with him a powerful remembrance of that day. (William Dealtry, in H. C. G. Moule, *Charles Simeon*, 1892.) *Simeon was buried in the vault at the west end of the Antechapel; the initials CS can be seen on the floor.*

1841 A. W. PUGIN: The moment the flat or four-centred arch was introduced, the spirit of Christian architecture was on the wane. Height or the vertical principle, emblematic of the resurrection, is the very essence of Christian architecture . . . and although some of the later buildings, as King's College Chapel, Cambridge, still retain the principle of internal height, with the use of the depressed arch, yet who can avoid being struck with the inconsistency of running up walls to a prodigious elevation, and then, instead of carrying out the principle, and springing a lofty groin, losing a considerable increase in height by a flattened thrusting arched ceiling; the form of which is a sort of contradiction to the height at which it is commenced. I do not make this observation by way of disparaging the merits of this stupendous building, but merely to show the early decay of the true principles of pointed architecture which may be traced even in that glorious pile. (*The True Principles of Pointed or Christian Architecture.*)

1843 ILL-TRAINED VOICES: Coming straight from the Abbey and from St Paul's, innumerable shortcomings of the choir at King's were painfully apparent to me. I am guilty of no exaggeration when I say that not one boy in the choir of sixteen could read his part at sight, or had any acquaintance with rules for the production of the voice, or had ever heard of phrasing, or was told to attend to marks of expression . . . The magnificent Chapel has a resonance which lends charm to any music performed under its lofty vault, quite independently of the artistic merits or defects of the performance. The voices of the six lay-clerks, half of them worn-out; the ill-trained or un-trained voices of the boys; these, supported by the majestic tones of the organ, produced an *ensemble* in that splendid building which satisfied the ears of uncritical listeners. (W. E. Dickson, *Fifty Years of Church Music*, 1894.)

1843 QUEEN VICTORIA AMUSED: She walked up the passage through the Antechapel (which was crowded on either side by elegantly dressed ladies, who heeded not 'a good squeeze' for the sake of a sight of the Queen, or maybe of the Prince) leaning on the Prince's right arm . . . It was quite evident that the moment they set foot within this noble building they were struck with admiration at its matchless beauty: their eyes were cast at once upon the elaborate roof, and involuntary expressions of surprise were heard to escape them. (*Cambridge Chronicle*, 28 October.)
During evensong Victoria occupied the chair formerly sat in by Queen

Elizabeth, on a canopied dais with its back to the altar. The service over, the aged organist John Pratt, persuaded to play for the last time in his career, thundered out Handel's 'Zadok the Priest' as the young Queen passed along to the west door, the Provost and Senior Fellows walking backwards before her, and occasionally stumbling as they trod upon their gowns. (W. E. Dickson, *Fifty Years of Church Music*, 1894.) *When she returned next day, the undergraduates lining the route* threw off their gowns, and laid them on the ground for Her Majesty to walk upon. This characteristic act appeared to amuse the Queen very much. (*Cambridge Chronicle.*) *Prince Albert later went on the roof.*

⚜ 1844　ANTHEM FOR A KING: As the King [Frederick Augustus II of Saxony] crossed the threshold of this magnificent fane, the swelling tones of the organ burst upon his ear in that noble monument of Handel's genius, the Coronation Anthem . . . He who cannot realize in his own heart King's Chapel in the glory of a bright sun, with Handel's music pealing from its organ, and a King at its gates, may hope for little aid to his fancy from our feeble pen . . . There was no mistaking the eloquent silence with which his eyes wandered over 'the fretted roof', while his ears drank in the strains of swelling harmony which dwelt lingeringly about. (*Cambridge Chronicle*, 22 June.)

In my youth I had once made a drawing of this church after a copper-plate engraving, and longed anxiously to see the original. Now it was before me – slender, lofty and light. As we entered the organ was played, and a very happy effect was produced by the sunlight subdued by the lofty stained-glass windows. Thus it is that many of our expectations in life are fulfilled with a surprising richness. (C. G. Carus, physician to the king, *The King of Saxony's Journey through England and Scotland*, 1846.)

👑 1847　WOULD WAKE A CLOD: It would be pre-eminent in the first city in the world . . . Twenty-five windows, each about fifty feet high, superbly adorned with painted glass, unite to shed a hue of gorgeousness, ever varying, on every portion of the interior, as sun or cloud prevails. There is a floating light around us, stone almost ceases to be stone beneath its influence . . . A powerful organ is here placed, and when its thundering notes are pouring forth, the spirit of the veriest clod seems awoke within him. (*The Pictorial Guide to Cambridge.*)

The view through the west doors (Ackermann, 1815).

❧ **1849** JOHN RUSKIN: King's College Chapel, Cambridge, is a piece of architectural juggling, if possible still more to be condemned [than Sta Sophia, Constantinople], because less sublime. (*The Seven Lamps of Architecture.*) *Ruskin omitted this passage from subsequent editions, because it* took no account of the many charming qualities [the Chapel] possessed through its faults, nor of its superiority to everything else in its style (1880). *However, on 6 April 1851 he wrote to his father that he had* got a glimpse of King's College Chapel, which I think uglier even than my remembrance of it; *and the following day,* I have not said a word too much against King's College, though it is a finer thing than any of the prints represent it. *Elsewhere in* Seven Lamps *he complained:* What a host of ugly church towers have we in England, with pinnacles at the corners, and none in the middle! How many buildings like King's College Chapel at Cambridge, looking like tables upside down, with their four legs in the air! . . . Knock down a couple of pinnacles at either end in King's College Chapel, and you will have a kind of proportion instantly.

♚ **1849** OVER-ZEALOUS: A work of destruction [is] going on in the magnificent Chapel of King's. The beautiful windows are being taken out and, after cleansing, replaced, at an average expense of £300 each. Instead of being restored, however, their beauty is being destroyed, much richness of colour is lost, and bad drawing evident, where new glass has been inserted in place of that broken in their removal. (*The Guardian*, 7 November.) *J. P. Hedgeland, the glazier responsible, protested that the loss is that of dirt only but his restoration, which had been going on for several years and had affected most of the windows in the Choir, was stopped. Hedgeland's Victorian replacements can be easily detected.*

❧ **1850** ALFRED TENNYSON
　　And heard once more in college fanes
　　　　The storm their high-built organs make,
　　　　And thunder-music, rolling, shake
　　The prophets blazoned on the panes.
(*In Memoriam* 87.)

♚ **1853** MATTHEW ARNOLD: King's College Chapel deserves all that can be said of it. Yet I feel that the Middle Ages and all their poetry and impressiveness are in Oxford and not here. (To his wife, 2 March.)

~~~~~~

❦ 1854 HACOMBLEN'S LECTERN: It stood broken in the library when I was young . . . When I was rich I had it done up by Skidmore, the best metal artist of the day in Church work; when mended it was set on an oak platform made by Rattee, of Cambridge, then the best carver of oak etc., for churches; then I had to pay Butterfield, the then best architect for High Church, £2 2s for a design of candlesticks for it; and then I had to get the candlesticks, and altogether it cost nearly £50, and it was worth it. (William Johnson Cory, *Letters and Journals*, 1897.) *See overleaf.*

♔ 1855 NOT MERE VITRIFIERS: These windows must ever be acknowledged to offer a truly wonderful collection of designs and details, worthy of a high place (yea, I submit, in the absence of anything more worthy, of the highest place) in our kingdom of historical art. The men who painted them were not mere vitrifiers or glaziers, but artists in a high sense of the term. Refreshed from the fountains which Michelangelo and Raphael had just opened to the world, they approached their material with no mean ideas or trembling hands; their arms seem to have forgotten the trammels of lead and of arming, and to have swept over the glass with grand and flowing lines, that can scarcely be outdone, and every bold contrast of colour and composition. (W. J. Bolton, *Archaeological Journal*.)

❦ 1860 DENTED CRINOLINES: If there was any inconvenient crush, it resulted in nothing more alarming than rents, easily mended, in very pretty dresses, and pardonable detriment to the symmetry of certain expansive contrivances, which it would have been far better on every account to have left at home upon such an occasion . . . On and on flowed the stream into the nave and the unreserved part of the Choir . . . 'The cry was still, they come' even after the avenues had got choked up by crowds apparently looking in vain for a resting place. Somehow or other, we really don't know how, people got gradually shaken down into their places . . . The number of persons accommodated in the Choir, exclusive of Fellows and attendants, was 1,374; and in the nave 1,940, making a total of 3,314. (*Cambridge Chronicle*, 26 May.) *The occasion was a Choral Festival inaugurating the rebuilt organ, at which Sterndale Bennett conducted a choir of 125 voices in a service with ten anthems. Nowadays the maximum seating capacity of the Chapel is about 1,750.*

⚜ **1860** LIFE MODELS: Two clumsy Gothic pinnacles which then surmounted the western towers [of the organ] were removed and the present angelic trumpeters set up in their place. An old member of the college once told me that in order to ascertain the size of the angels 'two slender youths' were sent up aloft to stand upon the summits while the authorities waited below to judge the effect. (Andrew Freeman, *The Organ*, January 1929.)

⚜ **1861** OFFER TO REBUILD: That wonderfully overpraised building, King's College, Cambridge . . . can hardly be placed before the architect as an example to be studied: the glass is good of its kind, so are the Renaissance west stalls and screen, while the roof is a pretty puzzle in stone-cutting: all the rest of the building is, however, positively bad, as far as I can judge. (William Burges, in *The Builder*, 23 March.) *Taken to task by a Cambridge correspondent, Burges offered to endeavour to convert him at Cambridge itself, by rebuilding his college Chapel, or indeed the chapel of any other college at Cambridge, for there are several which are in great need of it. (The Builder, 13 April.) In 1875 this most extravagant of High Victorian architects was commissioned to redesign the Chapel's east end. He prepared a characteristically elaborate scheme, involving painting the stonework and vault, and filling the niches with statues. It was rejected on grounds of expense.*

👑 **1863** OVERLOADED: Its architectural style is that known as the third pointed, or perpendicular gothic, and rich and florid though it be, it shows many tokens, in the depressed arches, the low gables, and the overloaded ornamentation, of the decline of the true principles of gothic art, of which it was one of the last, as well as one of the most sumptuous erections. (*The New Cambridge Guide.*)

⚜ **1866** RUSKIN REBUKED: I am willing that a thousand Oxford graduates should write books to prove that King's College Chapel is all wrong – that it extinguishes the Lamp of Truth (spelt with a big T) – and that it looks like a dining-table turned upside down. If so, all I can say is, *malo errare cum Platone* – I'd rather be wrong with King's Chapel than right against it. (William Everett, *On the Cam.*)

◀ *Provost Hacomblen's lectern before restoration (from* The Cambridge Portfolio, *1840).*

👑 **1867** DIVINELY GUARDED: A building reared amidst the most troublous times that England has ever known, and prosecuted under circumstances apparently the most unfavourable, yet over which a special providence seems to have watched, so that it has remained to the present day in a condition more perfect than any other great ecclesiastical building in this country, preserved alike almost wholly from the malice of wanton enemies and the zeal of injudicious friends, and guarded with a jealous care by those who have the good fortune to possess it. (T. J. P. Carter, *King's College Chapel: Notes on its History and Present Condition*.)

⚜ **1868** NE PLUS ULTRA: Upon entering King's College Chapel, [Ferdinand] David [the German violinist] was so taken aback by the beauty of the interior, that he seated himself and, after a few minutes silence, said with great seriousness: 'Bennett, you must let me stay here, I must see nothing after *this*.' Bennett's own love for the Chapel was so intense that his companion could not have touched a more responsive chord. (J. Sterndale Bennett, *The Life of William Sterndale Bennett*, 1907.)

᥉᥉᥉᥉᥉᥉᥉᥉᥉᥉᥉᥉᥉᥉᥉

⚜ **1876–1929** ARTHUR HENRY MANN: *The modern musical tradition at King's began with the appointment of Dr Mann as organist; in Provost Brooke's words he was the maker of the King's choir as England knows it.* During his 53-year tenure the King's College Choir School was re-established as a boarding school; the lay clerks were gradually replaced by choral scholars; the Christmas Eve Carol Festival was founded; and the music standard raised to its present pre-eminence. *His musical style, however, came later to seem unrepentantly Victorian. He took most music very slowly, and caused it to be sung with great deliberation and distinctness of enunciation. His accompaniment was inclined to be luscious, with passing notes and descants, and his extemporized preludes were wonderful pieces of colour and modulation, without any very precise development of form; but the result was that instead of a service being a performance in a building, the very building itself seemed to speak, with all its abundant echoes and lingering sweetness.* (*The Times*, 20 November 1929.)

Opposite: *Dr Mann on the roof, c.1916.* Below: *The choir, 1912. Dr Mann is in the second row from the back. Provost M. R. James is seated centre, with Eric Milner-White, instigator of the Carol Services, second from the right.*

⚜ **1879** HENRY JAMES: The effect it attempts to produce within is all in the sphere of the sublime. The attempt succeeds, and the success is attained by a design so light and elegant that at first it almost defeats itself. The sublime usually has more of a frown and straddle, and it is not until after you have looked about you for ten minutes that you perceive the Chapel to be saved from being the prettiest church in England by the accident of its being one of the noblest. It is a cathedral without aisles or columns or transepts, but (as a compensation) with such a beautiful slimness of clustered tracery soaring along the walls and spreading, bending and commingling in the roof, that its simplicity seems only a richness the more. I stood there for a quarter of an hour on a Sunday morning; there was no service, but in the Choir behind the great screen which divides the Chapel in half the young choristers were rehearsing for the afternoon. The beautiful boy-voices rose together and touched the splendid vault; they hung there, expanding and resounding, and then, like a rocket that spends itself, they faded and melted toward the end of the building. (*English Hours*, 1905.)

♛ **1879** THE WEST WINDOW: Stacey, in his speech, quoted the passage in the 'Holy Grail' where Tennyson – no doubt basing his description on a recollection of King's Chapel – describes a great Hall with a window at one end and twelve on each side 'blazoned', and one at the other end plain; and then the question is asked, 'Who shall blazon it?' Stacey declared that when he was an undergraduate and looked at the bare west window he determined – he must have anticipated in thought the poet, who did not write his Idyll till many years later – that, if ever he had the means, *he* would blazon it! (William Austen Leigh, *Augustus Austen Leigh*, 1906.) *The glass, designed by Clayton & Bell and depicting the Last Judgement, was paid for by F. E. Stacey, a former Fellow. Other traditions assert that he glazed the window in remorse for a youthful indiscretion: it was for long known as 'Stacey's Repentance'.*

⚜ **1880** CANDLES: Attending the 5 o'clock service at King's Chapel, he comments upon . . . the scene presented by the growing darkness as viewed from the stalls where they sat. 'The reds and the blues of the windows became of one indistinguishable black, the candles guttered in the most fantastic shapes I ever saw, – and while the wicks burnt down these weird shapes changed form; so that you were fascinated into watching them, and wondering what shape those wisps of wax would take next, till they dropped off with a click during a silence. They were stalactites, plumes, laces; or rather they were surplices – frayed shreds from those of bygone "white-robed Scholars", or from their shrouds – dropping bit by bit in a ghostly decay. Wordsworth's ghost, too, seemed to haunt the place, lingering and wandering on somewhere alone in the fan-traceried vaulting.' (F. E. Hardy, *The Early Life of Thomas Hardy*, 1928.)

1881 PEDANT REFUTED: I once heard a well-informed archaeologist observe that it was the misfortune of England in the middle ages, that while it had masons, it had, unlike France, no architects. We were standing in a window-recess in the first court of King's College. I made him no answer, but pointed to the Chapel which stretched its majestic length along the opposite side of the quadrangle. (George Gilbert Scott, *An Essay on the History of English Church Architecture*.)

1884 SEATED DURING ANTHEM: Sirs: A regular attendant at the afternoon services in King's Chapel can hardly fail to be struck by the larger and continually increasing proportion of ladies who remain seated throughout the anthem. A casual and charitable observer might attribute the phenomenon to a 'limb-relaxing' peculiarity of Cambridge air. But the activity and endurance which I have seen not a few of

The 'majestic length' of the south front, depicted by Le Keux, c.1826.

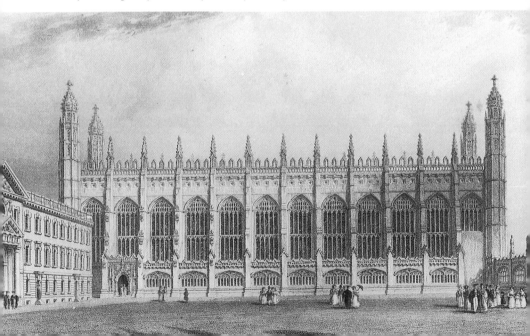

these ladies display in the ballroom or at lawn tennis seem to me incompatible with a great degree of physical weakness. No doubt the length of the anthem may be pleaded in their favour, but it is not an excuse for deliberately sitting down at the outset. (*Cambridge Review*, 5 November.) *Among several replies, only one protested that* for my part I do not see why any except the choir should stand during the singing of the anthem at King's, or elsewhere.

👑 **1884** ANARCHISTS: Stepping softly, I crossed the Chapel, and began to ascend the stair. The greatest caution was necessary, as the stair was steep and narrow, and the steps much worn. Further, I was in darkness, except where the loopholes through the tower wall lit up a few steps with a dusky light. When about halfway up, I remember vividly my foot kicking against a small fragment of stone, which went rattling downstairs. For a few seconds I stood breathless; but, hearing nothing, again went forward. A little further up I began to hear, very faintly, the monotonous chink of iron against stone. They were evidently at work, drilling into the roof. As I mounted higher the sound grew more distinct, and, on reaching the top of the stair, I could hear voices speaking low, and mingling with the sound of the hammer and chisel. The door into the passage was open. My position was a very dangerous one. ('A Lurking Danger: A Tale of King's Chapel', in *The May Bee*.) *The narrator, an antiquarian, was on the track of an anarchist plot to dynamite the vault during the May Week service. The story was possibly written by M. R. James, then an undergraduate at King's, later Provost.*

⚜ **1885** NOT LONG ENOUGH: King's Chapel, though far superior to that of Trinity as a building, is much inferior in point of acoustical arrangement and effect. The reverberation at King's is superabundant and most confusing to the auditor; often resulting in a mere chaos of rolling and stupefying sounds . . . If King's Chapel were twice the length, the echoes and confusion would not be one half as annoying. (William Glover, *The Memoirs of a Cambridge Chorister*.) *Glover, needless to say, had been a chorister at Trinity.*

👑 **1886** OLIVER WENDELL HOLMES: But beyond, above all the rest, the remembrance of King's College Chapel, with its audacious and richly wrought roof and its wide and lofty windows, glowing with old devices in colours which are ever fresh, as if just from the furnace, holds the first place in my gallery of Cambridge recollections. (*Our Hundred Days in Europe*, 1887.)

1886 FUNERAL: There was music as we entered the Chapel, which was carpeted with cloth for silence sake. We passed by the open vault which was strewn all around with flowers and moss, and followed the coffin into the Choir. I passed by it, going to my seat; it was fragrant with rich white flowers. After the service they sang the lovely anthem from Spohr's Last Judgement and a still lovelier one which Stanford had composed for the occasion. [Professor] Westcott and [Archbishop] Benson both took part in the service. The dead march was played again, and the choir sang very beautifully round the grave, whither we all went. After the coffin had been lowered and all was over I went to the edge of the vault and looked down the steps. It was a beautiful sight. The sides of the vault were draped with black, flowers were strewn around and down below in the dark but lit up with candles was the coffin groaning under its burden of wreaths. I stooped to the edge of the grave and picked up as a last token of the departed these symbol flowers. (C. R. Ashbee, Unpublished journal.)
The funeral was of Henry Bradshaw, University Librarian and Fellow of King's.

c.1887 MANAGEMENT OF CROWDS: On the most crowded Sunday afternoon in the May Week I went into Chapel and found the entrance into the Choir congested with a seething mob. A neighbouring magnate was repeating, 'But I'm Mr Pemberton of Trumpington', and the harassed servant in charge was saying: 'I don't care who you are, Sir, you can't come in without you've got an order'. Suddenly [J. E.] Nixon [the Dean] entered, hurried up to the crowd and proclaimed: 'Unless all of you leave the Chapel this moment, there will be no Divine Service this afternoon.' I am afraid the announcement did not produce the slightest effect. Nixon, however, was satisfied that he had coped quite successfully with the situation, and immediately wrote another hektographed pamphlet 'On the Management of Large Crowds'. (M. R. James, *Eton and King's*, 1926.)

c.1887 RIPPING! They sat on when the singing was done, while the remaining prayers were intoned, waiting for the crimson curtains in the entrance of the Choir to be drawn; then a flood of mellow candlelight poured out into the Antechapel, and as the organ muttered and

modulated into the key its master sought, the procession of singing boys and men followed by a few Fellows in surplices streamed out in pairs. David, always vivid in perception and emotional in mind, basked in the soft, solemn splendour of it all, and yet even while he absorbed and loved it, he couldn't help thinking of the silly line, 'The animals came out two by two – hurrah! hurrah!' . . . Then other animals came out one by one, for a verger with a silver poker preceded the Provost to the door. His bald head shone faintly like a moon in the candlelight . . . Hurrah! hurrah! How ripping it all was, and he wedged his shoulder against Frank's, for he must be in touch with him when he enjoyed himself particularly. (E. F. Benson, *David of King's*, 1924.)

1887 CLASSICAL: The really grandest building in late Perpendicular. Here the windows and the fan-tracery roof are of the very best kind, and the ornament throughout, though rich, is not overdone. And the design is as bold and simple as a Greek temple. (Karl Baedeker, *Great Britain*.)

1889 FLOATING EFFECT: Nothing, however, can compare with the tranquil enjoyment of a service in King's Chapel. It has been said that even a book let fall there will not fail to produce music. There is nothing in the acoustic proportions of the stately building to cause the slightest jarring impression. At the unaccompanied services on Wednesdays, one is more than at any other time struck with the peculiarly beautiful 'floating' effect of the voices, while the dim candlelight lends an additional charm, quite medieval in its character. (*Cambridge Review*, 14 November.)

1889–92 CHORISTER TRIALS: The least competent boys were generally those who brought a roll of music under their arms, and came prepared to give us 'O for the wings of a dove' with the full strength of the instrument, but were warded off, firmly, yet with no wounding of susceptibilities. In the end, five or six select boys would be taken into Chapel, and, to a somewhat larger audience, would each sing a hymn they knew. This would compensate for all the weariness of the morning: the child had ceased by that time to be nervous . . . and one was in no hurry to cut off the lovely sound. (M. R. James, *Eton and King's*, 1926.)

⚜ 1890 TWIN ANGELS

Twin angels guard the awful avenue, –
　　Vaulted infinity of shade –
That seems to stretch far on into the night,
　　Yea, on and through the night,
Until thou come to that great altar's steps,
　　Whereon thy life shall then be laid:
Twin angels – in their hand no sword of flame
　　But trumpets tipped with light.

('King's College Chapel', *Cambridge Review*, 19 June.)

♔ 1891 OUTRAGE: Four undergraduates immediately in front of me

spent the time in telling each other funny stories, to judge from ceaseless and undisguised laughter, and in tying each other to the backs of the chairs by the ribbons of their gowns . . . Behind these sat two ladies (?) who confessedly enjoyed the game, and also to all appearance much relished the ocular conversations with which the combatants, in their breathing spaces, favoured them . . . The service is attended by a crowd of undergraduates who make no pretence of caring either for religion, music or decency; and these are followed naturally enough by a crowd of the other sex, whose object is best left to conjecture . . . The authorities must do something, and do it quickly, if they do not wish to lose all the more reverential portion of their congregation together with their reputation. They would hardly wish their church overtly to serve the purposes of a Roman temple of Ovid's day. (Unpublished letter from an Oxford graduate to the *Cambridge Review*.)

⚜ c.1892 LOCKED IN: I was awakened by the south door banging to,

and discovered that I was locked in . . . There I sat. The moon was shining and I could see some of the figures in the windows, which pleased me, and I fixed my attention on that which represents Reuben looking at the empty well where he expected to find Joseph. To my horror I saw him, distinctly, lower his arms (which had been raised over his head in surprise), retire to the edge of the well, and sit down on it. Then he yawned – I heard him – and began feeling about in his drapery. Then he began to say something in a somewhat metallic tone which became more natural as he went on. 'Well, I suppose that feller Joseph as took and gorn off on one of his larks. I thought he worn't in that pit. And now for a pipe.' Yes – he said 'a pipe'. You may imagine my feelings when, apparently from the bosom of his red shirt, he produced an extraordinarily murky clay, filled it, struck a match on the stonework of the well, and lit up; so that soon an odour, as of the worst variety of shag, stole over the sacred edifice. (M. R. James, 'A Night in King's College Chapel', first published in *Ghosts and Scholars* No. 7, 1985.) *Evidently Reuben never resumed his gesture of surprise.*

👑 1893 CAMILLE SAINT-SAËNS: Each college has its chapel – nay, cathedral – and every day the students are present at service and sing, clad in surplices. This religious character of the English Universities is not their least curious aspect. Not that it is wearisome! Their services are very short and mainly consist of hearing good music very well rendered, for the English are admirable choristers. (*Portraits et Souvenirs*, translated in the *Cambridge Review*, 9 November.)

⚜ 1893–1906 WINDOWS RESTORED: A scaffold with many floors was put up, from which every part of the window could be got at with complete ease. This was moved from window to window as required. Great was the excitement, when a fresh window was thus made accessible, of going all over it, settling what mistakes must be rectified, what glaring modern patches should be taken out and replaced by neutral-tinted glass, and what ancient patches were worth removing and preserving; for it had been the habit of the eighteenth century repairers to stop up holes with pieces of old glass that they had by them, and some of these were of considerable beauty and interest. (M. R. James, *Eton and King's*, 1926.) *The fourteen windows untouched by Hedgeland (see 1849) were releaded and repaired at the rate of one a year by the glazier C. E. Kempe.*

👑 1894 WINDOWS PROSAIC: To me, there is very little effective religious expression in a great deal of the work. It is essentially prosaic in thought and strong and physical in drawing. Still, the pictures cannot be divested of the traditional beauties of composition and colour which were inherited by all artists educated in those days. (N. H. J. Westlake, *A History of Design in Painted Glass.*)

A close-up view of the fan vault, which Santayana describes as spreading like a canopy ▶
over a procession.

∾ ᏸ ∾ ᏸ ∾ ᏸ ∾ ᏸ ∾ ᏸ ∾ ᏸ ∾ ᏸ ∾ ᏸ ∾ ᏸ ∾ ᏸ ∾ ᏸ ∾

⚜ **c.1895** INSIDIOUS EMOTION: I couldn't bear the music there! I don't expect anyone to understand about this, but I simply hated the unfair, juicy way in which the organ notes oozed round inside the roof, and sapped your vitals, and made you want to cry about nothing at all. I liked my music dry, not wet, in those days, just as I still do. Dr Mann was organist then, and I dare say that he was rather soulful; at any rate, I have never yet been able to dissociate music at King's Chapel from the kind of emotional appeal which I find most antipathetic of all. (Gwen Raverat, *Period Piece*, 1952.)

♔ **c.1896** GEORGE SANTAYANA: From my front windows I could see the exterior of the Chapel in violent perspective, the buttresses standing in file, like soldiers with shields, lances and banners, or like the statue-columns of Karnak. Only a corner of the windows was visible at the top; above which the rough grey wall was crowned with lovely perforated battlements and pinnacles. Away with the pedants who say that battlements should not be perforated! . . . That which at once catches and

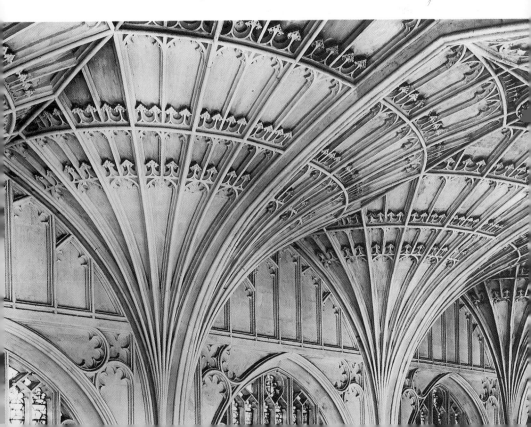

holds the eye is the vault. It is held up, lifted up, as if it could move, like a baldachino over a procession; it is woven of intricate fan traceries, undulating slightly, without sharp arches, or heavy pendants; the fans open like palm trees from the piers, and then merge their branches in a chain of diamonds and circles down the flat central part. It is regal elegance, rather than religious mystery, that spreads this canopy over us; yet never was perspective more magnetic or vault more alive. We are in the presence of something magical, something sublime. (*My Host the World*, 1953.)

⚜ 1898   INCOMPARABLE: These windows contain the finest series in the world of pictures in glass on a large scale. (J. W. Clark, *A Concise Guide to the Town and University of Cambridge*.)

♔ 1899   A PROVOST'S VIEW: To the uninitiated eye it might have been the creation of a single night; and in this respect it offers a contrast to most English cathedrals, which charm us by the varieties of their architecture as much as by their intrinsic beauty. It is interesting also as the meeting-point of the last Gothic with the earliest Renaissance work. And the effect produced by the combination of the great stone vault with the long line of rich glass is one which can hardly be felt elsewhere, except, indeed, at York Minster . . . Like other really great works, King's Chapel produces an impression which is instantaneous and at the same time permanent. (A. Austen Leigh, *King's College*.)

⚜ 1899   FINE BUILDING: On arriving we examined the Chapel. Loud were the exclamations of approval. Aunt Eliza repeated 'it is so sumptuous, so rich, the glass is so rich – like woven silk, so . . .' and she waved her hands. 'Fine building, remarkably fine building' kept on remarking Uncle Frank. (E. M. Forster to his mother, 10 November.)

♛ 1901   EVERYONE ANGRY: Thursday night was the Brahms Requiem in the Chapel, which I much liked. Oh the clacking men! never at peace, but always wishing to make their voices heard – for you wouldn't believe it, but nearly everyone in the college is angry because they have the Requiem in the Chapel. The Low Church people are angry because a Requiem is Popish, the High Church because it was on an Ember day, the Fellows because they hadn't got seats for nothing, the aesthetic people

∾ ᘓ ∾ ᘓ ∾ ᘓ ∾ ᘓ ∾ ᘓ ∾ ᘓ ∾ ᘓ ∾ ᘓ ∾ ᘓ ∾

because they said the electric light would injure the Chapel, the patriotic people because it was against the traditions. A letter has actually been sent by some undergraduates to the Visitor, the Bishop of Lincoln, complaining of it! (E. M. Forster to his mother, 2 March.) *The Requiem, to mark the death of Queen Victoria, was performed by a chorus and orchestra of 310.*

⚜ 1901   THE SCREEN: It has been called the finest piece of woodwork this side the Alps, and its exquisite design and workmanship quite justify the description, and even incline one to omit the limiting line . . . The general design and most of the work must have been done by Italians, and the whole screen must be regarded as an isolated example, complete in itself, not growing out of anything that went before it, nor developing into anything afterwards. (J. Alfred Gotch, *Early Renaissance Architecture in England.*)

A detail of the central doors of the screen, showing the Stuart royal arms – a 17th-century addition to the earlier carving, which is presumed to be by continental artists.

⚜ c.1904–08

CATHOLIC NOSTALGIA: Receiving the Cup at King's was like quaffing the Holy Graal. It was a sweet white wine: the *Lacrima Christi*. Edward felt he had received some vague initiation and walked back with folded hands. The colour of the glass transfigured his soul. Unknown sanctities and duties summoned him like clarion call. The Golden Legend surrounded and inspired him. Those wonderful windows had not been stained and emblazoned to feed the gaping tourist or to tickle the antiquarian, but to delight and lead the simple and youthful into the paths of righteousness. Edward was filled with a sense of indefinable mission . . .

In wonderful raiment the beams of the morning sun crept upon Edward's swooning eyes. Yellow and scarlet patches broke through the argentine glaze without a half-tint or a semi-tone to modify their clash. The sun's rays collected in the fine Venetian gold, in the fantastic flesh pinks and languishing rose, melting and emblazoning the glass to cyclamen and peach-blossom and heliotropic sanguine, but cooling into clotted clarets and the murrey hue of bull's blood. Slowly the sun stole along the Chapel like the face of a mighty dial, dwelling an hour upon each window and stirring blobs, blurs and blotches of glaucous greens, cinereal amethysts and gorgeous oranges, while the heraldry aloft blazed in asteriated sapphire and aureate sateen. All the trimmings of the original Deuteronomic rainbow preserved in amber! (Shane Leslie, *The Cantab*, 1926.)

⚜ 1905

THE 'SULTAN OF ZANZIBAR': At King's I watched the head porter, Nightingale, dash out to throw wide the great gates. Old Walter the Verger was summoned, but the Sultan as a Moslem declined to enter the Chapel, which was reverent and right, but through his interpreter he conveyed one immortal message to the college: 'What holy men must inhabit here!' (Shane Leslie, *Long Shadows*, 1966.) *The 'Sultan' and his entourage were students who had dressed up and hoaxed the Mayor into showing them round. They neatly avoided the impropriety of entering the Chapel wearing turbans.*

♔ 1905

SOLITARY AND ALOOF: On this splendid site of many acres, where now the silent green expanse of sunlit lawn has taken the place of the busy lanes and crowded tenements, which in Henry's time hummed with the life of a medieval riverside city, there rises the wondrous building, the crown of fifteenth-century architecture, beautiful, unique – a cathedral church in size, a college chapel in plan – seeming in its lofty majesty so solitary and aloof, and yet so instantaneously impressive. (Charles W. Stubbs, *The Story of Cambridge*.)

c.1905–12 SPY-HOLE: Now and then 'Daddy' Mann would invite my sister and myself to visit him in the organ loft, for Sunday morning service. This was an immense treat, and I would watch, and marvel at, the agility with which he tackled the intricacies of manuals, stops and pedals. Like a presiding deity brooding over the sounds below he would, at times, carry on a whispered running commentary on the service, and would dilate in low tones upon the standard of the singing. When he considered a passage of music badly rendered, he would groan softly to indicate his mental anguish, or mutter under his breath in condemnation. In the east side of the organ screen I found a small, round hole. This may have been a knot-hole and, whether by chance or by design, it gave one an excellent view of the Choir should one's eye be closely applied to it. This hole was, for me, the symbol of an unspoken wish. Here I was able to see much, without being seen myself. (M. A. Rowley, 'Memories of Childhood in Cambridge', in *The Fleur-de-lys*, No. 16, 1976.) *Mrs Rowley's father, T. C. Weatherhead, was headmaster of the Choir School.*

1912 PEACE: The great Chapel of St Martin's, planted like some couchant animal grey and mysterious against the blue of the evening sky, flung through its windows the light of its many candles. He found a seat at the back of the dark high-hanging Antechapel. He was alone there. Towards the inner Chapel the white-robed choir moved softly; for a moment the curtains were drawn aside revealing the misty candlelight within; the white choir passed through – the curtains fell again, leaving Olva alone with the great golden trumpeting angels above the organ for his company.

Then great peace came upon him. Someone had taken his soul, softly, with gentle hands, and was caring for it . . . From the heart of the darkness up into the glowing beauty of the roof the music rose. It was Wednesday afternoon and the voices were unaccompanied. Soon the *Insanae et Vanae* climbed in wave after wave of melody, was caught, held, lingered in the air, softly died again. (Hugh Walpole, *The Prelude to Adventure*.) *Olva Dune had just murdered a fellow student.*

〜〜 〜〜 〜〜 〜〜 〜〜 〜〜 〜〜 〜〜 〜〜 〜〜 〜〜 〜〜 〜〜

⚜ **c.1912** CHRISTMAS: It would be Christmas Eve: we of the college surpliced ourselves and repaired to Chapel. Choir and Antechapel were full, and dark. Just before the clock struck five the boys would issue from their vestry on the north side, the men from the Hacombleyn chantry on the south; last, the officers came from the Brassie chantry, and, led by Walter Littlechild with his silver verge, proceeded westwards and took their stand near the south door. A faint musical hum was heard, of the choir taking up the note, and then – it seemed to give the very spirit of Christmas – the boys broke quite softly into 'Once in Royal David's City', and began moving eastward. With the second verse the men joined in. I declare I do not know what has moved me more than this did, and still does when I recall it. (M. R. James, *Eton and King's*, 1926.)

No lapse of time, no change in custom, can rob those earlier carol services of their intrinsic beauty. Whether this beauty was spiritual or aesthetic in its appeal, the same intangible quality held us spellbound; an enchantment that no modern method of broadcasting or televising can fully capture or rediffuse . . . My mother took my sister and myself into the Antechapel, where we sat in tranquil semi-darkness on the rearmost seats, our backs almost touching the west wall . . . There was a lovely simplicity in the form of service that would seem to have become partially lost in these days of greater publicity. (M. A. Rowley, 'Memories of Childhood in Cambridge', in *The Fleur-de-lys*, No. 16, 1976.)

♔ **1914** WOULDN'T QUITE DO: Easter Sunday, April 12. I decided to go to King's – sate in the Antechapel . . . A few imbecile, wild, officious people in the nave; one woman eyed a small book in her hand hungrily and intently, and sang wolfishly; a foolish elderly man handed about books; a young man talked and giggled to a young woman. The music was very characteristic – hymns with tubas, like streams of strawberry jam, and gliding intermediate chords, gross, like German cookery. As for the service, there was no mystery about it, or holiness – it was no more holy than a Union Jack – it was loud and confident. But old Smart in F was charming enough, a strange mixture of levity and sweetness. Altogether it wouldn't quite do; it was very beautiful both to see and hear, but had no wisdom or depth about it. I had no impulse at all to pray or weep. And yet one must not neglect the fact that people come together for it, sit through it gravely, without smiling – even believe in it! (*The Diary of Arthur Christopher Benson*, ed. Percy Lubbock, 1926.)

✣ 1914 HIGH DIVE: A terrible fatality occurred last month . . . Mr A. H. Sadd, whose curiosity shop opposite the college was one of the oldest businesses in Cambridge, appears to have climbed to the top of King's College Chapel in a dense fog, and to have thrown himself down, under the impression that he was diving into the river. This appears to be the only explanation of the tragedy, and Mr Sadd was well known as a keen swimmer and a very frequent figure at the bathing sheds. (*Cambridge Magazine*, 10 October.)

♔ 1914–18 VALUES SUSTAINED: And sometimes when I slipped into King's Chapel after a weary parade, and sitting at the back, let my eye wander over its roof full of shadows cast by the candlelight, while the voices of the choir floated down it as if from some region where all discord was dissolved in adoration, the vicious preoccupations of the afternoon, the self-important efficiency of those who were instilling into me the elements of military discipline, their insistence that a rifle should be the prime object of a soldier's devotion and that a bayonet should be handled with the skill and determination of a butcher – all seemed an unendurable violation both of the beauty and sanctity of life and of my essential being. (Hugh I'Anson Fausset, *A Modern Prelude*, 1933.)

✣ 1918–41 MASTER OF CEREMONIES: *Perhaps the greatest of Deans of Chapel, Eric Milner-White reorganised the services, founded the Festival of Nine Lessons and Carols (1918) and the Advent Carol Service (1934), donated or caused to be donated much stained glass, rehabilitated four of the side-chapels for worship, and brought to the services a heightened element of significant movement and colour.*

> Milner-White
> Looks well by candle-light;
> That's why
> We have our service High.
> (*Basileon*, 1928.)

Now we know why the Dean is such a lover of ballet; he is the best choreographer of us all. (The ballerina Lydia Lopokova, after attending a Carol Service.)

A famous recent Director of Music, Sir David Willcocks, with the choir in the 1960s.

1918 THE CAROL FESTIVAL: This service, after ancient precedent, was revived by Archbishop Benson for use in Truro Cathedral, the Lessons, which tell the whole story of our Redemption, being read in order by the Cathedral ministers from chorister to Bishop. In this Chapel it is adapted to symbolise and express the loving bond between the two Foundations of King Henry VI here and at Eton, the goodwill between University and Town, and peace within the Whole Church of the Lord Jesus, as well as the joy and worship of us all at the coming of our Christ. (Order of service.) *The Festival of Nine Lessons and Carols has been sung every Christmas Eve since 1918, and broadcast on the radio every year since 1928 (except 1929). A televised version was first shown in 1954.*

1919 RUDYARD KIPLING
Hallowed River, most gracious Trees, Chapel beyond compare,
Here be gentlemen tired of the seas – take them into your care.
('The Scholars'.) *Four hundred former naval officers, whose education had been interrupted by the War, were allowed to study temporarily at Cambridge.*

👑 **1922**　**V**IRGINIA WOOLF: They say the sky is the same everywhere . . . But above Cambridge – anyhow above the roof of King's College Chapel – there is a difference . . . Is it fanciful to suppose the sky, washed into the crevices of King's College Chapel, lighter, thinner, more sparkling than the sky elsewhere? (*Jacob's Room.*)

⚜ **1923**　**B**EETLES SACRED AND PROFANE: Mustchin of Corpus . . . explained that his only interest in King's Chapel lay with insects in the pigeon-muck between the vault and the roof. 'I have found the Pope's Tick there, the yellow and white bug that bites worshippers in Canterbury Cathedral,' he mentioned amid laughter. 'Death Watches and Devil's Coach Horses and weevils live on the Chapel roof as well.' 'It sounds jauntily irreligious,' said Professor Gow, 'but you might write a paper on Beetles Sacred and Profane.' (Shane Leslie, *The Cantab*, 1926.) *In fact a paper on the Chapel's animal ecology had been published by A. D. Hobson of Christ's and L. H. Matthews of King's. Apart from pigeons, they found a barbastelle bat, a snail, numerous spiders, little pseudo-scorpions or false-scorpions, mites, the pigeon tick referred to by Mustchin (yellow and white being the papal colours), hibernating Peacock and Small Tortoiseshell butterflies, the larvae of various moths, various beetles including the Devil's Coach Horse, swarms of flies and fleas, and lice, bugs, and silver-fish.* (Annals and Magazine of Natural History, XI, 1923.)

👑 **1925**　**T**. E. LAWRENCE: The splendiferous college with the extra-splendiferous (and rather horrible) Chapel. (To E. Palmer, 10 December.)

⚜ **1926**　**F**LICKERING SHADOWS: Evening service on a late autumn Sunday in King's Chapel is a ceremony not easily forgotten. Nowhere is religious emotion more artfully induced than by the successive baths of darkness and colour and light and sound through which the worshipper passes . . . Candles set upon the stalls and seats are the only lighting, and the tenuous candelabra and canopies of the stalls are full of flickering shadows. All Kingsmen wear long surplices, the choir the scarlet cassocks of the chapels royal, and candlelight, cast upwards on white linen, begins to fascinate the unaccustomed eye. At first the stranger can divert his attention to the huge coloured windows and the interlacing circles of the vaults. But as twilight without deepens into night, the stories in the glass fade, the saints and emperors and ships and cities imperceptibly lose colour, and, with colour, shape. The roof disappears. Far away to the east, across a piece of night, the high altar shows a few yellow points. But at length eye and mind are imprisoned in the little sea of candlelit surplices rustling like luminous golden foam in a canyon of blackness. Nothing else in the world has reality but the melodious liturgy. (Christopher Hussey, *King's College Chapel, Cambridge*.)

1929–57 A PERFECTIONIST: He was tyrant and friend . . . There was never a hint of relaxation in the standard expected. With his keen sensitiveness to pitch and musicianship, it is doubtful whether any performance ever quite satisfied him. We were certainly left with the impression that, whatever our achievement, Boris could always imagine something better. When, after a mighty rendering of Charles Wood's *Collegium Regale* evening service and a magniloquent anthem, the exhausted choir returned to the vestry, how often would Boris come padding round to dispel our exalted pride with the quiet 'thank you', as to someone who had just passed the salt, and to criticise the pitch of the final 'Amen'. Boris would not perhaps have described himself as a religious man, yet there was a quality about all that he did in Chapel – even practices were never secular – which suggested that to him only the very best was fit for the worship of God in that place. (Eric Hall, choral scholar 1932–5, in Philip Radcliffe, *Boris Ord 1897–1961*, 1962.) *Bernhard 'Boris' Ord succeeded A. H. Mann as organist.*

1929 CRABS AND CRAYFISH: It was amusing enough to watch the congregation assembling, coming in and going out again, busying themselves at the door of the Chapel like bees at the mouth of a hive. Many were in cap and gown; some had tufts of fur on their shoulders; others were wheeled in bath-chairs; others, though not past middle age, seemed creased and crushed into shapes so singular that one was reminded of those giant crabs and crayfish who heave with difficulty across the sand of an aquarium. (Virginia Woolf, *A Room of One's Own*.)

1932 UMBRELLAS *ET AL*: Cambridge people were astonished yesterday to see two open umbrellas securely fixed to the two pinnacles on the west end of King's College Chapel. One umbrella was eventually brought down by a shotgun. (*The Times*, 19 May.) Roof climbers were again busy at King's College Chapel, Cambridge, on Monday night and fastened a full-size Union Jack on the north-eastern pinnacle of the building. From that pinnacle to the centre pinnacle [*sic*] a wire was slung, from which is now suspended a bottle of wine. The umbrella fastened on the pinnacle at the other side of the Chapel last week is still there, though in a very bedraggled condition. (*The Times*, 25 May.) *The shotgun owner refusing to fire on the Union Jack, a steeplejack had to be employed.*

❧ **1933** EDGE OF DECADENCE: I can criticise King's Chapel now. I can see it as the expression in stone of a spirit that in aspiring upwards had already lost something of its true centre of equilibrium, that had begun to indulge in a decorative excess and to tremble upon the edge of decadence. The structure is too exquisite. In some lights it is hard even to believe that it is of stone and not some shadowy image of the dreaming mind or some climbing melody which has assumed momentarily a visible form. It has the ethereal quality of Beethoven's last quartets, but the strange, heartbreaking discords which we feel constantly being resolved in Beethoven's music, are wanting to it. For those who built it were pursuing beauty a little too much as an end and yearning rather too exclusively for infinity's embrace. (Hugh I'Anson Fausset, *A Modern Prelude*.)

♔ **1934** NULLIFIED: A precipitous wall of stone and glass . . . tending by its very size to nullify itself when it has become familiar and to enter but little into the general consciousness of the college. (E. M. Forster, *Goldsworthy Lowes Dickinson*.)

⚜ **1937** A CHALLENGE: Climbers always look at it with awe and reverence. It has a fascination about it which will not let the mind rest. The severity of its aspect is a challenge, a coaxing invitation one minute and a stern rebuff the next. It is possible to grow to love the Chapel, seeing it reflected in every face, hearing the singing of its pinnacles in every storm of wind, thinking of it many times during the day and dreaming of it by night, having only to cast back to it to return to a higher world of thought and feeling . . . Those who have seen it outlined against the sunset or the full moon, those who have seen its sloping leaded roof-top glisten after a shower of rain, those who have looked down upon the world from its

Traversing a turret; from The Night Climbers of Cambridge *(1937).*

summit, all those who have seen these things will remember the poetry that it has taught them. ('Whipplesnaith' [Noel Howard Symington], *The Night Climbers of Cambridge*.)

♔ **1939** TAR-PAPER: On 1 September 1939, when the Germans invaded Poland, a telegram had gone out to the holidaying members of the Council asking their consent to the removal to safety of the east window of the Chapel. Seven others were also removed during the Michaelmas term. Then there was a pause until the war heated up in the summer of 1940. By the end of 1941 all the ancient windows had been removed. Their rectangular sections were stored in the cellars of Gibbs' and in other cellars in Cambridge and elsewhere. They were replaced by sheets of grey tar-paper, with occasional horizontal strips of plain glass at the bottom to let in light. The west window of 1879 remained, appreciated at last in the absence of unfair competition. But the Chapel was colder than ever in the winter, and the tar-paper rattled thunderously in the wind. (L. P. Wilkinson, *A Century of King's*, 1980.)

I suppose they were wise though I sometimes wonder what they will do with the windows if the Chapel is demolished. (A. S. F. Gow, 29 September 1940, in *Letters from Cambridge*, 1945.)

⚜ **1939** AIR RAID PRECAUTIONS: In the possible event of an Air-Raid Alarm sounding during the service, 1) The congregation near the three doors at the west end of the Antechapel should stand well clear of them in order that they may be thrown open as widely as possible by the Chapel officers. 2) People in the Antechapel who desire to go out and seek shelter should do so as quietly as possible, without haste or pressure. 3) No person in the Choir should move unless or until a responsible college officer gives instructions. (Order of service, Christmas Eve.)

♔ **1943** NIKOLAUS PEVSNER: To design this long, tall, narrow box of a college chapel, no spatial genius was needed . . . They were rationalists, the men who designed and enjoyed these buildings, proud constructors, of a boldness not inferior to that of the Catalans. Yet they succeeded . . . in combining this practical, matter-of-fact spirit with a sense of mystery and an almost oriental effusion of ornament. Standing at the west end of the Nave one can hardly think of the supreme economy with which this effect of exuberance has been attained. (*An Outline of European Architecture*.)

❖ 1943 **JOHN BETJEMAN:** Evening light in the Chapel with the colours dying in that forest of Tudor stone and glass and the distant choir filing out of the candle light and high, high above us the complicated roof – not even Wordsworth's sonnet does justice to this most exquisite interior. (*English Cities and Small Towns.*)

♛ 1948 **SIR WINSTON CHURCHILL:** Clapping and cheering followed him all the way down the Passage and round the corner to King's. The Chapel was over three-quarters full before the music chosen for the occasion, Purcell's Coronation Anthem, was due to begin. The three choirs of King's, Trinity and St John's were at their most impressive. (*Cambridge Daily News*, 10 June.) *The occasion was the traditional performance of the 'Chancellor's Music' to mark the installation of a new Chancellor of the University, Field Marshal Smuts. Churchill was among those present to receive honorary degrees.*

⚜ 1948 **UNACCUSTOMED WHITENESS:** Anyone revisiting King's College Chapel, Cambridge, for the first time since the cleaning of the interior was begun is bound to experience a shock on going inside. The unaccustomed whiteness of the stonework for the first few moments is startling, and the glass, now replaced in the majority of windows and also cleaned, is found to have gained an unfamiliar translucency and brilliance of colouring. . . . The truth is that few realised how dirty everything had become, roof, walls and windows. We had almost persuaded ourselves to believe that dirt and stains were the hallowed patina of time. (Arthur Oswald, *Country Life*, 26 November.)

♚ 1951 **ROYAL THANKSGIVING:** As first the car containing Princess Margaret and then that in which the King and Queen travelled passed over King's Bridge on arrival at the college, boys from the college choir school . . . raised a cheer which was taken up by the crowd lining the route to the west door of the Chapel. There the Provost and Fellows waited to receive the royal visitors. (*Cambridge Daily News*, 28 April.) *The occasion was a service of thanksgiving for the preservation of the Chapel during the War and the restoration of the glass. The Archbishop of Canterbury gave the blessing.*

The royal visitors leaving the Chapel with Provost J. T. Sheppard, April 1951. ▶

⚜ **1952** ENTENTE CORDIALE: The supreme English example of what the later medieval artist tried to construct – a temple that fairly glitters . . . Judged as a whole – sound, stone, wood and glass – this Chapel is bad to beat; even an Englishman need not be ashamed of saying so, while gratefully remembering foreign elements in the plan. (Kenneth Harrison, *The Windows of King's College Chapel*.)

♔ **1952** E. M. FORSTER: King's College Chapel, whatever our reactions to it, is an incomparable building. There is nothing like it in Christendom or in the world. It triumphs through three mediums: stone, glass, wood, and in the presence of that sumptuous trinity criticism is often dumb. Overwhelmed by the greatness of the enterprise and by its smashing success, the visitor sinks on to a rush-bottomed chair and gapes. Here is colour and form and atmosphere. Here perhaps are sounds. Later on other feelings may supervene: something may seem missing for the very reason that so much is present: a small imperfect country church may hint at

possibilities ignored by this proud Tudor corridor . . . Even if one finds it lacking in the numinous, one has no doubts as to its greatness. It is one of the great buildings of the world, and it is unique. If it perished, no millionaire and no government could replace it. (*The Listener*, 29 May, reviewing Kenneth Harrison's book.)

❧ **1954** EFFECTS ANALYSED: [Wastell's] heightening and elaborate finishing of the four corner turrets may be criticised for giving them an undue emphasis and altering, not for the better, the proportions of the exterior as a whole; and the openwork parapet, graceful though it is and well related to the tall pinnacles, gives a frilly finish, teasing to the eye on a building of such length. The fan vault, which is the glory of the interior, depends largely for its effect on the succession of strongly emphasised transverse arches, breaking up the compartments and providing just the right contrast to the spider's web of the vault itself. (Arthur Oswald, *Medieval English Architects*.)

♛ **1954** 'SUNDAY MORNING, KING'S CHAPEL, CAMBRIDGE'.

> File into yellow candle light, fair choristers of King's
>   Lost in the shadowy silence of canopied Renaissance stalls.
> In blazing glass above the dark glow skies and thrones and wings
>   Blue, ruby, gold and green between the whiteness of the walls;
> And with what rich precision the stonework soars and springs
>   To fountain out a spreading vault – a shower that never falls.
>
> The white of windy Cambridge courts, the cobbles brown and dry,
>   The gold of plaster Gothic with ivy overgrown,
> The apple-red, the silver fronts, the wide green flats and, high,
>   The yellowing elm-trees circled out on islands of their own –
> Oh, here behold all colours change that catch the flying sky
>   To waves of pearly light that heave along the shafted stone.
>
> In far East Anglian churches, the clasped hands lying long
>   Recumbent on sepulchral slabs or effigied in brass
> Buttress with prayer this vaulted roof so white and light and strong.
>   And countless congregations as the generations pass
> Join choir and great crowned organ case in centuries of song
>   To praise Eternity in time and coloured glass.

(John Betjeman, *A Few Late Chrysanthemums*.)

*** 1956 SUICIDE: It was a Saturday night in 1956, when I was vicar of the University Church, Cambridge. I had been asleep for two or three hours when I awoke with a sense of horror. I was so frightened that I turned on the light. One thing was clear to me – I must call on the Dean of King's College as soon as possible. I got up early and arrived at the college gates soon after 8 a.m. I was met by the porter, who said that the Dean had committed suicide during the night by throwing himself from the turret of the Chapel. (Bishop Mervyn Stockwood, *The Times*, 2 May 1969.) *Ivor Ramsay, Dean of Chapel since 1948, had climbed the south-west tower in the middle of the night and fallen 90 feet to his death. Ian Stephens, a Fellow with rooms on the adjoining staircase in Gibbs' Building, recorded in his autobiography* (Unmade Journey, 1977) *how he too had a psychic premonition of the tragedy.*

*** 1957 'KING'S COLLEGE CHAPEL'
When to the music of Byrd or Tallis,
　　The ruffed boys singing in the blackened stalls,
The candles lighting the small bones on their faces,
　　The Tudors stiff in marble on the walls,

There comes to evensong Elizabeth or Henry,
　　Rich with brocade, pearl, golden lilies, at the altar,
The scarlet lions leaping on their bosoms,
　　Pale royal hands fingering the crackling psalter,

Henry is thinking of his lute and of backgammon,
　　Elizabeth follows the waving song, the mystery,
Proud in her red wig and green jewelled favours;
　　They sit in their white lawn sleeves, as cool as history.

(Charles Causley, *Union Street*.)

*** 1957 SYLVIA PLATH: I caught a passing rainbow in a pastel arc over the tiny town of Cambridge, where the spires of King's Chapel looked like glistening pink sugar spikes on a little cake. (To her mother, 8 February.)

*** 1959 WINDOWS DEPLORABLE: The well-known sixteenth-century windows in King's College Chapel ... are evidence of the new mental outlook in which the art of the glazier has been completely subordinated; that of the painter predominates. However much the technical skill in painting may be justly admired, it is impossible not to deplore the complete lack of architectural appreciation or understanding of the material they were using. They have lost the beauty of glass in a triumph of chiaroscuro and perspective, a gallant but misguided attempt to imitate oil painting. The artist no longer strove to depict religious truths with piety and sincerity but rather revelled in an exhibition of materialistic effect which would have been appropriate to a town hall or other secular building but which, in a Christian church, was fundamentally an exhibition of bad taste. (E. Liddall Armitage, *Stained Glass: History, Technology, and Practice.*)

⚜ 1961   THE RUBENS: During the year the College has received the gift of a work of art of the very first rank . . . In March 1961 the Provost received a letter from Mr A. E. Allnatt, asking whether the College

would accept the picture and place it in the Chapel. Mr Allnatt's intention was to preserve it for all time in this country and to restore this major work of religious art to some great ecclesiastical building – and of all buildings which he inspected with this end in view he felt that King's Chapel was the most fitting. (King's College, *Annual Report*.) *Rubens' Adoration of the Magi was painted in 1634 for a convent in Louvain. It was brought to England in the 1780s and belonged to the Grosvenor family from 1806 to 1959, when Major Allnatt, a retired property millionaire, bought it at auction for £275,000, then a record price. In 1961 it was installed temporarily in the Antechapel while the college considered how best to integrate it with the Chapel. In 1964, after the removal from the sanctuary of the reredos and panelling (mostly installed by Detmar Blow in 1911; but some of the panelling was the work of Cornelius Austin, the 17th-century carver who made the canopies over the stalls), the painting was moved to the east end. The present arrangement dates from 1968.*

♔ 1962   YEVGENY YEVTUSHENKO: After lunch we went across to King's Chapel . . . In the way he looked about him I thought I detected the courteous interest, the concern to see but not to make comparisons, of a man looking at something impressive that the Other Side had done.

'You atheist?' he asked me in English.

'Well yes, but it's more that I hate him.'

I felt he understood me very fully. He gave his delightful grin . . . 'Me,' he said, pointing to himself, then gesturing more vaguely towards the roof, the other people there, the Rubens, but also seeming to include the being I had just mentioned; 'me . . . means nothing.' (Kingsley Amis, *What Became of Jane Austen? And Other Questions*, 1970.)

⚜ 1962   QUEEN ELIZABETH II: After being surrounded by cheering crowds at Addenbrooke's Hospital yesterday, the Queen spent twenty minutes in the quietness of King's College Chapel. She spent much of the time admiring the great Rubens *Adoration of the Magi*. All the doors to the Chapel were closed so that she could see the floodlit painting to its best advantage . . . Slowly the Queen walked through the Chapel. (*Cambridge Daily News*, 29 May.)

◀ *Installing the Rubens at the east end, April 1964. The picture is painted on wood and requires a steel frame to support it.*

🜲 **1963** TRANSCENDENT: King's College Chapel, in particular, is the one Gothic building that has commanded consistent and unqualified praise from every critic from the sixteenth century to the present day, transcending every change in architectural taste as the plays of Shakespeare have transcended every change in literary fashion . . . It represents the final simplification of collegiate church planning, and shows that English Perpendicular was capable of achieving a unified design as satisfying in its way as any imposed by the discipline of the classical orders. (*The History of the King's Works*, ed. H. M. Colvin.)

⚜ **1964** SECULARITY CONFOUNDED: Within are seen heraldic beasts, diadems, and the giant fungus of the Tudor rose on a scale to dwarf a sunflower; for after a century of political delays, the structure was finally accomplished in the reign of Henry VIII, and the prodigious emblems of his royalty usurp the credit of a Plantagenet foundation and even, perhaps, a little of the Almighty . . . But what with the stone cobweb of the fan-vaulting above the Antechapel; the organ case like the poop of *The Great Harry* jutting midway into an indoor sky; the tapers burning at evensong, remote, in the Choir; and by day the subdued dazzle of tremendous windows – Elijah rapt to heaven and letting fall his scarlet mantle of prophecy, Christ walking in the Easter garden and 'holding a spade as if to give colour to Mary's mistake' – inexorably, and with a slow magnificence, the balance of sacred and secular is overtipped and the pomp of things terrestrial forgotten. (Christopher Hassall, *Rupert Brooke: A Biography*.)

🜲 **1965** YEHUDI MENUHIN: It was one of the most perfect musical occasions I can remember, in Cambridge or anywhere else. Everything was entirely right. The great resonance of the building acted as a natural amplifier of the violin's tone . . . The echoes gave an added richness to the sound without blurring it. I realized, for the first time, that a highly resonant building is just the place to hear solo violin music. In a 'dead' building it can sound unbearably dry, so that one is acutely conscious of the lack of accompaniment. In King's it sounded self-sufficient, almost orchestral at times . . . As Menuhin stood alone in the dim candlelight, his face pale and his features blurred, giving out his magical sounds, one was reminded of the fabulous Paganini . . . It was an unforgettable experience. (Nicholas Temperley, *Cambridge News*, 9 February.) *Menuhin's Bach recital was in aid of Oxfam.*

❧ **1965** 'PEACE IN VIETNAM': A banner calling for 'Peace in Vietnam' flutters from the spires of King's College Chapel today, following a daring and dangerous night climb by students. Three students took 75 minutes to shin the 147 feet to the top of the spires. *The danger was heightened by crumbling stonework and the students wrote anonymously to the Dean that* unless work is effected immediately the safety of future climbers of your Chapel is in grave jeopardy. (*Cambridge News*, 7 June.)

♚ **1968** SECOND MAJOR RESTORATION: *The Chapel was closed for nearly a year while its interior was cleaned, the organ overhauled, the Choir repaved, electric lighting and a new underfloor heating system installed, an entrance for concert crowds made on the north-east side, and the east end rearranged with the Rubens for altarpiece. The architect was Sir Martyn Beckett. The Chapel reopened in December 1968.*

If there is a certain loss of [the] numinous, there is certainly aesthetic gain. At the same time certain questions must be asked, because King's College Chapel is not just a private place of worship: it is a national institution . . . This painting now takes the place of the Empty Cross. Is this

The east end before alteration in 1968, with reredos, panelling and ritual steps.

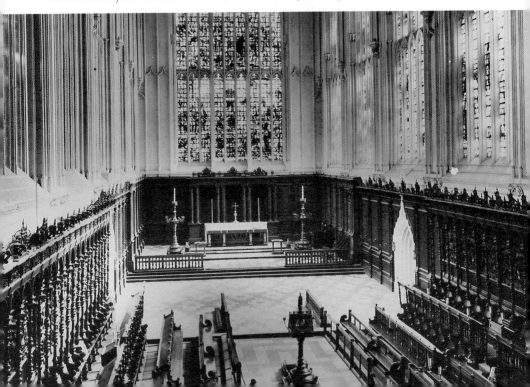

a symbol of secularisation? (Canon Hugh Montefiore, *Great Saint Mary's Newsletter*, December.)

It was found necessary by the architect of the scheme . . . to clear away all the beautiful panelling, which was introduced only some sixty years ago, but which after four centuries at last gave the sanctuary the warmth and life it had always craved. The Chapel now reverts to frigidity. (Hugh Plommer, *Cambridge News*, 19 December.)

The restored Chapel at King's College is magnificent but I feel that if the Rubens was moved to the right, say as far as the Fitzwilliam Museum, it would look even better. (Arthur Thair, *Cambridge News*, 19 December.)

⚜ 1969 IS GOD AT HOME? Halfway between Jehovah and Mammon stands King's College Chapel. Symbol of Cambridge, virtually functionless, enormously expensive. It was built in an Age of Faith (a long time ago), for the glory of God. The people of Cambridge built it for us. Now, for the largest number of Cambridge people, it is a once-a-year carol service on T.V. Visited only by some exclusive choir boys and tourists. Most Cambridge residents have never been inside . . . Of course there is the ever-present tinkle of the cash register as tourists reach for Serve-Yourself goodies, records of the exclusive choir, glossy pictures, instant histories, etc., BUT NO THUNDER! I hereby, satanically, suggest that an examination be made immediately to find out if God is still at home in the Chapel (a writ of Habeas Corpus Christi served on the priest in charge) and in the event that He can't be found, King's College Chapel be forthwith turned into an international supermarket so that we may derive some benefit, be it never so temporal. (Bill Powell (for Satan), *Cambridge Voice*, January.)

👑 1970 CLASH: It is powerful, vociferously dramatic, and painted in Rubens colours, i.e. colours which have no relation whatsoever with the colours of the marvellous stained glass of the Chapel. It may be a superb picture in its own right, but if any building in the whole country was not made for it, it was King's College Chapel . . . Now there is the never-ceasing clash between a strong architecture of which sculptural decoration and stained glass are an integral part and an isolated but very large Baroque object. (Nikolaus Pevsner, *Cambridgeshire*, 2nd edition.)

The present east end, with the Rubens as altarpiece, the floor levelled, the panelling removed, and light fittings (designed by Sir Martyn Beckett) on the walls. ▶

⚜ **1974**   VANDALISM: Deep grooves forming the letters 'IRA' on the surface of Rubens's *Adoration of the Magi* in King's College Chapel, Cambridge, may never be removed entirely by restoration, the Rev. Michael Till, the Dean, said yesterday. The damage was noticed by a visitor on Saturday after police had been called to investigate the robbery of an offertory box by thieves who broke in the previous evening. (*The Times*, 17 June.) *The Rubens, which is painted on wood, was successfully restored, but security was stepped up.*

♔ **1974**   GEOMANCY: This was the last temple in England to be built entirely to the Geomantic schemata, handed down from antiquity as the Cosmic Measure – a scheme uniting Man with the Macrocosmos, carefully executed in the correct manner, overriding politics, civil war and dynastic changes. (Nigel Pennick, *The Mysteries of King's College Chapel*.)

⚜ **1974**   TOURISTS' PROMENADE: Increasingly we are preoccupied with the growing number of visitors. The Chapel Clerks have a difficult time seating those who come to services, recovering service books that somehow tumble into handbags, sweeping up cigarette ends, iced lolly papers and other *detritus*; directing parents with hopping children to the nearest public lavatory, answering questions and restraining the sheerly presumptuous, e.g. the man who removed all the altar furniture so that he could take an uninterrupted picture of the Rubens, and the tour organizer who settled his followers to eat their sandwiches in the Choir. Visitors who have seen the Chapel as anything other than a promenade for jaded tourists owe that in large part to the work of these members of our staff. (King's College, *Annual Report*.) *During 1985 there were some 750,000 visitors.*

♛ **1982**   APPEAL AND ANTI-APPEAL: In name it is still the private Chapel of a College, but it is accessible to hundreds of thousands of visitors a year and shares its music and liturgy with congregations which may include 5000 people a week as well as with millions more through television and radio. (King's College Chapel Appeal leaflet.) *The Appeal raised £1 million to pay for the completion of the restoration of the external stonework (begun in 1973) and to provide a fund for future maintenance.*

Dear Readers! Please do not give *any* money to the King's College Chapel Appeal except on express condition that the panelling is put back, the floor